THE LAST OF THE PHANTOMS

Compiled and written by
Ian Black

Foreword by
Air Chief Marshal Sir John Allison

Patrick Stephens Limited
AN IMPRINT OF HAYNES PUBLISHING

First published in 2002

British Library Cataloguing in Publication Data
A catalogue record for this book is available from the British Library

ISBN 1-85260-612-6

Title-page badge: The 'Phantom Man' or 'Spook', designed by McDonnell Douglas and well known to Phantom crews.

Patrick Stephens Limited is an imprint of
Haynes Publishing, Sparkford,
Nr Yeovil, Somerset, BA22 7JJ.

Typeset in 10/14 pt Sabon.
Typesetting and origination by
Sutton Publishing Limited.
Printed and bound in England by
J.H. Haynes & Co. Ltd, Sparkford.

Contents

Phantastic Phantoms.

Dedication

This book is dedicated to the memory of two Phantom pilots. Both were fighter pilots in every respect and both were very dear friends.

Reg Hallam

Reg Hallam (below, left) was my squadron commander on 19(F) Squadron and I had the privilege to be crewed with him. A former test pilot and experienced Phantom pilot, Reg was one of the old school. Leading by example he was a delight to fly with. A superb aviator, he would never be flustered by anything that happened and his cool approach to flying remains with me to this day. A legendary war-bird pilot, Reg died in 1999 after a long illness.

Guy Bancroft-Wilson

A lifelong friend, Guy was a natural fighter pilot who flew the Phantom with gusto and skill. He blossomed during his time on the Phantom force and later became the RAF solo Hawk display pilot and then served in the Red Arrows. He joined British Airways in 1996, and soon became a captain flying the Boeing 737. An accomplished war-bird pilot, Guy was tragically killed flying the P63 King Cobra in June 2001.

I dedicate this book to the memory of these two fine aviators. 'One day we'll touch the blue blue sky.'

Phantom in the blue.

Foreword

by Air Chief Marshal Sir John Allison

In the early 1980s I was Station Commander at Royal Air Force Wildenrath, home to 19 and 92 Squadrons, both equipped with Phantom FGR2s. Those units were part of the 2nd Allied Tactical Air Force and contributed to the air defence of what was then West Germany.

On 3 February 1983 I would have died in Phantom XV497 but for the vigilance and presence of mind of my young, inexperienced first tourist navigator. In those days we rarely flew other than at low level and on this occasion we were tooling along at the usual 250 feet and 420 knots when the nav. suddenly shouted, 'Push'. One doesn't normally push at 250 feet, and certainly not much, but such was the urgency of his tone that I pushed anyway. A heartbeat later a dark grey shape flashed across the canopy, so close that we could hear and feel the shock of its passage, and I felt sure that it must have taken our fin off. It was a Jaguar, also going about its lawful business; the pilot clearly never saw us and, although he did not know it, he too owes his life to my navigator. That young navigator was Flying Officer Ian Black, the author of this splendid book.

At the end of his tour on 19 Squadron, Ian was selected for pilot training and went on to fly Lightnings in the closing years of that magnificent aircraft's service. Before flying the Mirage 2000 with the French Air Force, Ian ended his flying career with the RAF as a Tornado pilot, thus becoming one of the fortunate group of aircrew who flew all three types of aircraft that have provided the UK's air defence capability since 1960. This book is about what was incomparably the best warplane of the three – the Phantom.

The Lightning was perhaps the most exciting airframe, but its built-in fuel shortage, meagre weapons load and pulse radar limited its operational effectiveness. The Tornado is a good low-level bomber, but the F3 fighter variant, although latterly redeemed to some extent by a modern suite of weapons, sensors and communications systems, has insurmountable limitations as a fighter for the very reason that its airframe and engine design were optimised for the bomber role. That is disappointing, considering that the original design concept – and sales pitch to the MOD – was that it would be a multi-role combat aircraft. Indeed, before the aircraft was named Tornado, it was known by the acronym 'MRCA'. The reality is that the F3 replaced in the air defence role the Phantom, one of the few true multi-role combat aircraft the world has ever seen.

I recall taking part in one of the early RAF Tactical Fighter Meets at Leuchars in 1974. Admittedly, this was the heyday of the Phantom, but it was nevertheless remarkable that, of all the participating aircraft types, the Phantom was the only aircraft that was flown in every tactical role – air defence, strike attack, conventional attack and fighter recce. Moreover, the Phantom was also the dominant aircraft in each role. If you were flying Phantoms in the 1970s you were king of the skies.

The Phantom was the aeroplane of my life. I loved everything about her. She was not conventionally beautiful, but there was beauty in her proportions and in the flow of her purposeful lines, as is apparent from some of the stunning photos in this book. I enjoyed the comradeship and effectiveness of the two-man crew concept. Once one had mastered the Phantom's idiosyncratic handling, it was deeply satisfying to fly her on the edge of the manoeuvre boundaries more or less by feel, without the dubious benefit of digital intervention. Few aircraft have a more distinctive character. In truth, there is much that was not very good about her. For example, few pilots – especially fighter pilots, whose stock-in-trade is limit manoeuvring – would vote for a high wing loading, loads of adverse yaw, marginal longitudinal stability and poor stick force and positional cues. But overall the Phantom in its day was immensely rewarding to fly because, with ample power, fuel and weapons, a two-man crew and a pulse Doppler radar, it had real operational capability.

For those who never had the pleasure and privilege of flying the Phantom, the stories and photographs in this book are full of authentic insights that capture the experience. For those of us who knew and loved the Phantom, it is a nostalgic journey by which we can recapture some of the most exciting and satisfying experiences of our lives. Foremost among the memories that Ian has stirred for me is his treatment of the closing chapter of the Phantom's RAF service. It is remarkable how much one savours what is about to be lost and 1992, the last bitter-sweet year of the Phantom, burns all the more vividly in my mind from reading *The Last of the Phantoms*. Coincidentally, the last of the RAF Phantoms was actually XV497. I delivered her to her final resting-place at Coningsby on 31 October 1992, thereby closing, with great personal regret, a chapter in my own life as well as in the history of the RAF.

Air Chief Marshal Sir John Allison.

Introduction

Never the most glamorous of fighters, the Phantom nevertheless earned itself a reputation as a thoroughbred in every respect. Its performance in the Vietnam conflict is legendary, and it excelled in every role it took on. Its service with the Royal Air Force and Fleet Air Arm was equally illustrious, and it became the backbone of the UK defence forces for nearly a quarter of a century. Few aircraft in the history of the RAF have accomplished so much. It was a fighter-bomber, armed recce aircraft, nuclear strike vehicle and pure interceptor, long before the term 'multi-role' was invented. Flying the Phantom was never easy, but pilots quickly grasped the aircraft's idiosyncrasies, and once mastered it became a formidable fighter. Navigators had to cope with the most complex weapon system of its time. Indeed, with modern automation there may never be so complicated a weapon system to operate in the future. Groundcrews worked outrageous hours keeping the Phantom where it belonged, in the air. Never designed to be reliable, it was conceived in an era where manpower was plentiful. Respected by those who flew it and feared by those who fought it, the Phantom legend lives on today around the globe.

Having produced the critically acclaimed *The Last of the Lightnings*, it was indeed an honour to produce a similar work on my first fighter type, the ubiquitous Phantom FGR2. As a 21-year-old I spent three years riding the biggest fun machine the RAF possessed, and low-level air defence was the biggest rush of all. My passion for photography began when I was flying backseat in this most charismatic of fighter planes and it is for this reason that I hold it in such affection. My association with the mighty Phantom carried on for a further eight years after I left the Phantom force. Initially I became a Lightning pilot and then transferred to the Tornado interceptor. Some of my best flying was in the late 1980s and early 1990s 'fighting' the mighty F4, then in the twilight of its service. With plenty of fatigue to use up before their premature demise they were more than a match for the vapid fin (Tornado F3).

I am indebted to many people for their assistance in the preparation of this book. I'm especially grateful to Sir John Allison for writing the foreword: I could wish for no better person. I owe a great debt to all my fellow-pilots in Germany, not just for putting up with my photography but for the wealth of knowledge they passed on to me as aviators. Andy Neal, Phil Willi, J.G., Mike Roe, Fish, Rooibos and Lester Jackman are a few who spring to mind. I owe a mountain of thanks to Barry Dogget, Officer Commanding 56 (Firebird) Squadron and his crews. My thanks also go to Cliff Spink, then boss of the Tiger 'J' models, who kindly allowed me one last ride in the back. In particular I thank Group Captain (retd) Dave Roome who always seemed to find me a photo ship to immortalise the moment. There are many others, too numerous to mention, but I am deeply grateful to them all. Lastly I must thank the crews who kindly contributed their Phantom experiences to add to this work. My time on the Phantom lasted a mere three-and-a-half years, barely scratching the surface of the legend. My aim was always to capture the Phantom on film for future generations to enjoy. Some 25 tons of living, breathing, fire-spitting aggression, the Phantom always was and always will be a legendary fighter.

Ian Black
19(F) Squadron
RAF Wildenrath 1981–4

Heavy metal meets hard rock. No. 19 Squadron Phantom XV480 (B) cruises the Norwegian coast at low altitude.

CHAPTER 1

The Phantom Story

Ian Black

Like many aircraft that entered RAF service in the period 1950–80, the Phantom was an aircraft that should never have been. Its entry into service was to say the least via a rather circuitous route. In the early 1960s the Fleet Air Arm operated a mixture of ageing Scimitars and Sea Vixens in the ground-attack and air defence roles. The Buccaneer was then entering service, leaving the twin-boomed, twin-crewed Sea Vixen as the fleet's only dedicated fighter, but its antiquated radar and lack of a decent missile system meant the Navy needed a replacement fighter by the mid-1960s. At the same time the RAF was operating Hunters and Canberras in the attack role with Javelins and Lightnings in the air defence role. In an ideal world the simplest solution would have been for the two forces to adopt the same multi-role aircraft, but that would have been a very tall order indeed in the constantly changing early 1960s. The RAF suffered badly in the defence cuts of the 1957 White Paper although the Navy emerged relatively unscathed. What did survive, however, was the brilliant (on paper) Hawker P1154 Mach 2 VSTOL fighter. This would have been the most cost-effective answer to both the RAF's and the Navy's requirement for a fighter-bomber replacement. However, it was not that simple. The Navy wanted a twin-seat, carrier-borne fighter capable of long range and able to sustain supersonic speeds. The RAF wanted a single-seat strike aircraft capable of a supersonic burst of speed, and fitted with terrain-following radar, and (importantly) it had to have an in-service date of early 1968.

In February 1963 the government announced the P1154 as the RAF's Hunter replacement with the P1154RN (Royal Navy) selected for the Fleet Air Arm. At this stage both the Royal Navy and the French Aeronavale had shown a tentative interest in the McDonnell Douglas F4B Phantom and the Chance Vought F8 Crusader. Both aircraft had been trialled at the Paris air show in the early 1960s but in the event both were placed on the back-burner as work progressed on the futuristic P1154.

By 1964 the gap between what the RAF needed and what the Navy wanted became too large and the P1154RN was cancelled. The Navy said that the project was becoming too lengthy and too costly but the cancellation meant that there was no replacement for the charismatic but ageing Sea Vixen. The Navy had little choice but

Classic Phantom pose. XV480 (B) returns to its home base at Wildenrath after a low-level mission on the North German plain. Typical of the period (mid-1980s), the aircraft retains the old style grey and green camouflage.

Airborne! A clean-wing gun-armed FGR2 blasts off Akrotiri's main runway for a gun-firing sortie.

to look at the American Phantom as a potential successor to the Sea Vixen. With the Navy now accepting the much-improved S2 Buccaneer, thought was given to maximising the development costs of the Buccaneer by using the same Spey engine in the Phantom. In the meantime the RAF persevered with the supersonic P1154 until the new Labour government cancelled the whole programme. Within a short space of time the RAF lost the P1154, the TSR2 and the proposed purchase of the F-111. In their place it was decided that the RAF would purchase the American Phantom, powered by Rolls-Royce Spey engines and fitted out with British avionics. Thus the Navy and the RAF would at last have a common fighter. The plan was that the RAF would introduce the Phantom into service initially in the strike/attack role until the Jaguar was able to replace it. This would then free up sufficient airframes to allow the Phantom to replace the early Lightnings.

The British government was to become the first overseas customer for the F4 with an initial order for 140 F4Ks and 182 F4Ms. The Navy placed their initial order on 1 July 1964, requesting enough aircraft to supply its new carrier, a replacement for the obsolete HMS *Ark Royal*. Once again, however, politics reared its ugly head and the RAF's order for 322 Phantoms was slashed to 52 F4Ks and 118 F4Ms.

On paper the anglicisation of the all-American Phantom was fairly simple. Martin Baker would supply the twin ejector seats; various British companies would either build components or supply avionics; and Rolls-Royce would produce a reheated version of the Spey engine already in use with the Buccaneer. The tried and tested J79 turbojets would be replaced in the UK Phantoms with a pair of 12,500lb dry and 20,500lb reheated Rolls-Royce Spey 201 turbofans. In addition to the extra power, the Spey was thought to offer more bleed air for the boundary layer control, which would permit slower approach speeds. This would, however, mean that the air intake area would need to be 20 per cent larger and the rear lower fuselage area would have to be

It was unusual to see Wildenrath Phantoms in the clean-wing configuration as 2ATAF Phantoms were always gun-armed for an immediate response. Air combat phases gave the engineers a chance to remove the gun and drop tanks. It also allowed pilots to handle a more responsive machine.

Mission complete. One of the nicest things about flying the Phantom was cracking the canopy open when taxiing back to the line.

redesigned. Ferranti would look after the Westinghouse radar and fit an inertial navigation computer for the RAF FGR2s only. Interestingly this Inertial Navigation computer had been intended for the ill-fated TSR2 programme. Initially the Navy order was based on the US Navy F4B version. However, by this stage McDonnell Douglas at St Louis were forging ahead with an improved variant, the F4J. This was the most similar to the UK Phantom, but because of the small size of the British carriers the Navy aircraft would need modifications, including a slotted stabilator and larger flaps. Additionally the radome would need to be hinged to allow full opening through 180 degrees. This reduced the British Phantom's length to 54 feet. To improve take-off performance the British Navy aircraft would have an extendable nose-leg that would allow a full 40 inches of travel. This modification was tested on a US Navy F4B aboard USS *Forrestal*. Additional changes meant that RAF aircraft would not be fitted with hydraulic outer wing fold mechanisms. One of the prerequisites of the UK Phantom deal was that 40–45 per cent of the airframe should be produced in the UK. By the time the British had put their mark on the American Phantom the two air arms were getting an aircraft which bore little resemblance to its American roots. It was perhaps largely due to the fact that both the RAF and UK industry were unhappy about the choice of aircraft that so much was changed on the UK version. In particular, from the outset the marriage of Spey and Phantom was not a happy one.

The initial contract was for two prototypes designated YF4Ks (XT595 and XT596) and two pre-production F4Ks (XT597 and XT598). The two YF4Ks were hybrid aircraft powered by Speys but fitted largely with US equipment. XT595 first flew on 27 June 1966 at St Louis, with XT596 following two months later. They were both quickly dispatched to Edwards Air Force Base for engine trials. By 1 November 1966 pre-production aircraft XT597 had also taken to the air.

The Phantoms were designated FG1 by the Navy, meaning they were capable of both fighter and ground-attack duties. Production machines were fitted with Spey 202/203 engines. Compared to the J79 the Spey offered a 10 per cent increase in operational radius, 15 per cent greater range and better take-off performance. But it lacked speed and its performance at high altitudes left a lot to be desired.

The engine bay area needed major reworking in order to accommodate the bigger Rolls-Royce engine. This had a knock-on effect that would plague the British Phantoms during their early service. By the time of the first British Phantom flight on 27 July 1966 costs had soared and the unit price per airframe was well above that of the pure US variant. With the British Navy ultimately only forming one operational squadron (892 Sqn), most of the F4Ks went straight to the RAF. No. 892 Squadron formed on 21 March 1969 and spent that summer aboard USS *Saratoga* getting carrier-qualified. RAF deliveries began in 1968 after a first flight some twelve months earlier. Interestingly this was a time when the McDonnell Douglas war machine was at its peak, producing seventy-two aircraft a month, and the Phantom was proving its mettle in the Vietnam War some

Reg Hallam, then OC 19(F) Squadron, closes up on the Battle of Britain Memorial Flight's Spitfire Mk II P7350. At the time it wore the code QV-B, as used by 19 Squadron's Spitfires during the war. This squadron was the first Spitfire unit at Duxford in the late 1930s.

'Morning Glory.' In the twilight of its autumn years the 19 Squadron flagship awaits the day's flying programme. When this shot was taken at Wildenrath the squadron had but a few weeks to go before disbanding and re-forming as a Hawk training unit. This particular Phantom was almost at the end of its life as well. It was finally delivered to a museum in Czechoslovakia. Evident on the wing are the numerous strengthening patches applied to the upper surfaces.

distance away from Great Britain. In the end circumstances dictated that only twenty-nine Phantoms were delivered to the British Navy. The cost of refitting HMS *Eagle* for Phantom operations had proved prohibitive and a disastrous on-board fire left HMS *Victorious* uneconomic to repair. This left just one suitable aircraft carrier, the ageing HMS *Ark Royal*.

On 1 July 1965 it was announced the RAF would receive an initial order of 2 YF4Ms and 150 F4Ms. To begin with it was hoped that the RAF would purchase 200 airframes, but this figure was ultimately cut to 120 production F4Ms. Paradoxically the RAF would have preferred to buy the F4 with the original J79 turbojets but was persuaded to stick with the Navy option of Spey 202/203s. The first two aircraft, XT852 and XT853, flew at St Louis in early 1967. XT852 was then sent to Holloman AFB for trials while XT853 went to NAS Patuxent River.

All RAF aircraft were initially delivered to the maintenance unit at RAF Aldergrove in Northern Ireland prior to acceptance. Flown across the Atlantic by American civilian ferry pilots, they began to arrive in large numbers in 1968 and 1969. Deliveries were rapid and by 29 October 1969 the RAF's last Phantom, XV501, had been delivered. One late delivery was XV434, which

Looking into the cockpit of FGR2 XV430. This dirty-looking machine was one of the original air defence grey aircraft painted in a matt finish. Consequently it picked up every scuff and grease mark going and it's obviously due for a repaint. It has already had some cosmetic work done to the radome.

This is the same aircraft viewed from the lead aircraft during a pairs landing. The giant nosewheel oleo is evident. Also clearly shown are the leading edge 'blown' flaps and the high nose attitude.

Britain's finest. Six English Electric Lightnings are overshadowed by three McDonnell Douglas Phantom FGR2s. It was rare to see the two aircraft together and this shot was taken during the change-over period during an armament practice camp at RAF Akrotiri. The Lightning was a magnificent war machine but it was totally outclassed by the capable F4.

didn't arrive in the UK until 16 June 1970. It was delayed for repairs after an accident. The last Navy FG1 (XV592) was delivered on 21 November 1969.

Training for RAF Phantom crews was carried out at RAF Coningsby in Lincolnshire. No. 228 Operational Conversion Unit, formerly the Javelin OCU, was reformed in February 1968 and its first aircraft, XT891, arrived from Aldergrove on 23 August 1968. By the end of that year the OCU had some twenty aircraft on strength. Initially the OCU's task was to train crews for the recently reformed 6 Squadron, nicknamed 'The Flying Can Openers'. The pilots of 6 Squadron had previously operated the venerable subsonic Canberra bomber, but in one step they now had an aircraft that could fly at Mach 2, drop 16,000lb of bombs and tote an awesome arsenal of air-to-air weapons in the shape of radar-guided Sparrows and infrared Sidewinder missiles. For the first time the RAF had a potent bomber that could tote a full war load *and* carry air-to-air missiles. Additionally, when fitted with the EMI recce pod, the Phantom was one of the most advanced reconnaissance platforms in the world. The pod was equipped with cameras, infrared line scan and sideways-looking radar. It also housed mapping and moving target indication capabilities, which was highly advanced for its day. At last the Phantom had arrived. Ironically, its entry into service came at about the time the RAF would have been receiving the supersonic P1154. With the OCU busy training ground-attack squadrons, 43 Squadron began accepting FG1 (F4K) aircraft originally earmarked for naval use. These were to be air defence machines only. In some respects they were well suited to the role of holding

Northern QRA, as they didn't need to wait for the lengthy process of aligning the inertial platform before taxiing. However, once outside the range of conventional navigation beacons all they had was a very basic air computer of limited navigational accuracy. As 43 Squadron had taken on fourteen Phantoms deemed surplus to Navy requirements it seemed appropriate that the Navy (767 Squadron) should train the RAF crews. In fact the Navy continued to train its own crews until they finally gave up fixed-wing operations in 1978. Despite not having a fixed-wing force the Navy was still assigned two squadrons for ship defence: both 43 and 29 Squadrons were dedicated fleet defence units. They were assigned to SACLANT (Supreme Allied Commander Atlantic) in the TASMO (Tactical Air Support of Maritime Operations) role, thus effectively replacing the lost Navy squadrons.

A former Hawker Hunter unit, 43 Squadron was soon up to operational strength. Its aircraft, based at RAF Leuchars, were soon adorned with the famous black and white chequerboards and fighting cock emblems. As training progressed apace on the OCU the RAF entered a new era with the two-man crew concept. The two men had to work in perfect harmony in the F4 to achieve the maximum potential of this awesome war machine.

By July 1970 228 OCU had become 64(R) Squadron, a unit which had previously operated the Javelin all-weather interceptor. Training focused primarily on the ground-attack role. There were three squadrons based in the UK

Overleaf Cyprus was a favourite posting for air defence Phantoms for many years. A mix of red- and black-tailed Wattisham Phantoms gleam in the summer sunshine, 1992.

Perfect plan form . . . this is the 92 Squadron 'Blue Phantom' flown by Rick Offord, shown in an unusual clean-wing fit with a grey baggage pod. Since its paint job it has obviously gained a new port main wheel door.

XV488
T

XV422

Andy Walton tucks the gear up on XV400. Bound for the ranges, December 1983, the aircraft carries an ACMI pod on the right winder station.

A Phantom stands on the runway at RAF Valley, February 1983.

(nos 6, 41 and 54) and four more in Germany. Nos 14, 17 and 31 Squadrons were at Bruggen, while further up the road 2 Squadron was engaged in photo recce. By the mid-1970s the Phantom was already at the heart of the UK defences. At sea the FG1 was performing admirably while on land the FGR2s were engaged in every conceivable task from air defence to photo recce. As planned, the Phantom's role as a ground-attack platform was short-lived. First to go was 54 Squadron on 23 April 1974. The aircraft and some of its crews transferred to 111 Squadron, which had previously flown the English Electric Lightning F Mk3. The Phantom was entering a new era as an air defence fighter – a role that would see the aircraft take its place in the history of the Royal Air Force. By the end of 1974 29 Squadron, 111's sister unit at Wattisham, had taken over 6 Squadron's F4s. Next to follow were 23 and 56 Squadrons, leaving just two operational Lightning squadrons in the UK. The Phantom was now firmly on the map as the UK air defender. Leuchars operated 43 and 111 Squadrons with a mix of FG1s and FGR2s. Coningsby had the OCU and 29 Squadron and Wattisham had 23 and 56 Squadrons. Once the transition from Lightning to Phantom was complete in the UK, focus turned to RAF Germany where the Lightnings of 19 and 92 Squadrons had reigned for over ten years. By now fairly long in the tooth, the F2As of the Gutersloh-based Lightning squadrons were soon outclassed by the much more capable FGR2s. The Lightning had just two air-to-air missiles (Firestreak), limited to around 1.5 miles' range in the stern hemisphere. The radar was pulse only and virtually useless in the low-level environment. Pilots flying at low altitude would fold the radar away and try to 'skyline' their targets, relying on the Mark 1 Eyeball – the Lightning's best weapon system at low level. The Phantom was a tremendous leap forward in this respect, with a pulse Doppler radar that could detect targets at ranges of 30 miles at 250 feet (terrain permitting). A radar-warning receiver and an inertial navigation system were deemed essential for overland intercepts in a hostile environment. And most importantly the Phantom offered an enormous increase in firepower. First to form was 19 Squadron, whose aircraft largely came from 2 Squadron, then in the process of re-equipping with the single-seat Jaguar. No. 19 Squadron received its first aircraft in September 1976; 92 Squadron soon followed and by January 1977 both units were set up at their new home at RAF Wildenrath. The move had come about when the short-range Harrier force moved to Gutersloh to be closer to the East German border.

Once all the planned squadrons had equipped with the Phantom one would have expected a period of calm and consolidation throughout the force – but in reality there was no peace for the Phantom force. During the late 1970s and early 1980s aircraft were regularly sent back to the British Aerospace facility at Holme-on-Spalding-Moor for rework and modification. Top priority for the air defence role was the fitting of the fin-mounted Marconi radar warning receiver. This gave the British Phantoms a new look with a squared-off and enlarged fin tip. At the same time the aircraft were fitted out with instrument landing system (ILS) equipment. Other improvements included radar upgrades and a reliability package, as well as Sidewinder expanded acquisition mode. Throughout its career the F4 suffered from fatigue problems in both RAF and Navy service. This was hardly surprising as it was no agile lightweight fighter, although it was often flown as such. A particular problem was the outer wing area. One aircraft of 29 Squadron was lost when the outer wing folded during DACT (Dissimilar Air Combat Training) with a Canadian forces F104. Consequently

'Firebirds'. All-grey Phantoms wait for their crews on the line at RAF Brawdy in the winter of 1992. Before the application of red tails the 56 Squadron Phantoms were some of the least colourful F4s around.

Touchdown. XV439, the original 'A' minus the characteristic RWR fitting, lands firmly on Wildenrath's runway 27. In the background are the Bloodhound missiles pointing East – always a familiar feature.

Rick Offord reefs his clean FGR2 skywards, playing follow-my-leader high over the Yorkshire Dales.

many of the upgrades focused on beefing up the airframes, many of which had already spent several years in the punishing low-level strike role and were feeling the strain.

When the Royal Navy gave up its fixed-wing force its remaining FG1s were handed over to the RAF. In order to keep all the FG1s located at the same base 111 Squadron reconverted to the FG1 in 1978 using ex-Fleet Air Arm machines. The last Phantom launch from HMS *Ark Royal* was on 27 November 1978, after which all of 892 Squadron's aircraft were flown to RAF St Athan for rework to RAF standard. Externally the only visible differences from the FGR2 were the slotted stabilator, a small gauge on the rear fuselage to check the stabilator position and the three lights on the nosewheel door. For some reason the FG1s delivered to the UK were not able initially to carry the externally mounted SU23/A Gatling gun. This weapon was considered essential for air defence operations and all FG1s were subsequently retrofitted. Although 43 Squadron had been tasked with providing an aircraft and crew for the solo F4 slot in the summer aerobatics seasons, it was 56 Squadron which hit the headlines. In the spring of 1979 two Phantoms, XV424 and XV486, were painted in a special colour scheme at RAF St Athan to commemorate the first crossing of the Atlantic by Alcock and Brown in 1919, sixty years earlier. Using a standard squadron Phantom the RAF was able, by extraordinary coincidence, to crew the F4 with men named Alcock and Brown. (Backseater Norman Brown(e), a former Phantom navigator, was actually serving on a Buccaneer squadron but was brought back for the occasion.) Painted in special anniversary markings XV424 left the Canadian military airfield at Goose Bay on 21 June 1979 – exactly sixty years to the day since Alcock and Brown had crossed the Atlantic. Not wishing to re-enact the rather less glamorous aspects of the first crossing, the Phantom crew avoided crashing into an Irish bog and landed instead at RAF Greenham Common in time for the International Air Tattoo. The first crossing had taken 16 hours and 28 minutes; with the help of a Victor tanker the Phantom completed its crossing in 4 hours and 45 minutes. While 43 Squadron flew the display circuit the two specially painted Phantoms could be seen stealing

In this artistic study of the 19 Squadron anniversary jet (1915–91) it is easy to see how much the British Phantoms differed from their American cousins, with their new radar warning receiver, enlarged engine bay and ILS aerials.

the limelight at several air shows around Europe. Fortunately XV424 is preserved to this day at the RAF Museum, Hendon, although its sister machine XV486 was scrapped at the end of the Phantom era.

When Britain became involved in the conflict in the South Atlantic the one thing that the defence chiefs wanted was not available. *Ark Royal* had been scrapped and the Navy was operating the Sea Harrier – a far cry from the awesome firepower available to a joint Phantom/Buccaneer force. Very soon the RAF realised that it would be possible to deploy the Phantom down south once the Falklands were recaptured. The establishment and deployment of the Phandet warrants a book in itself, but suffice to say that by September 1982 29 Squadron had set up shop with four aircraft a very long way from the UK ADR. The need for a permanent air defence presence on the Falkland Islands led to the decision to transfer the squadron number plate to 23 Squadron, largely because 29 Squadron was one of the two UK squadrons allocated to SACLANT, or ship protection. With the Cold War at its zenith and the UK ADR one squadron down, a replacement for the deployed 23 Squadron was urgently needed. Attrition losses and the lack of spare airframes meant it would not be possible to deploy in-use ready reserves. The only option left for the RAF was to buy or lease a replacement fighter. While every self-respecting fighter pilot hoped for early F15As every full-blooded navigator wanted the F14 Tomcats due to be sold to Iran. In the end common sense prevailed (?) and more

A 92 Squadron F4 at the holding point. These F4s were among the most colourful: a vivid mix of reds, yellows, greys and greens.

O
P
L
E
N
XV473
H
X
XT903

F4s were sought. With the bone-yards at Davis Montham bulging with Phantoms it seemed a simple task, but, as with all things Anglo-Phantom, nothing was ever easy. The US Navy was now operating the F4S variant, an improved version of the old F4J. Optimised for carrier operations, these were of little use to the RAF. Instead the RAF had to make do with fifteen of the last remaining J models still in store and the US Navy began the task of putting these veteran fighters back into shape. Delivered to the UK in the last quarter of 1984 the F4J(UK) entered service with the much-respected 74 ('Tiger') Squadron. This time the Phantoms retained everything American, even down to the aircrew's flying clothing. Painted in an unusual grey-green colour, they were a welcome addition to the UK air defence network. Despite the fact that the F4J(UK)s were true American fighters one essential modification was carried out to the weapon system enabling them to carry the BAe Skyflash missile. In fact no sooner had the F4J entered service than the Phantom's replacement began to appear on the scene. The Tornado F3 had a troubled introduction to service but by 1987 the F3 had taken over from 29 Squadron as the first ADV (Air Defence Variant) unit. With the Tornado OCU setting up at Coningsby the long-standing 228 OCU moved north to Leuchars, enjoying less congested airspace. While the Tornado was replacing the Lightning in service the Phantom soldiered on at Wattisham and Leuchars. A new air defence base was built at Leeming and some radical changes took place in the dwindling Phantom force. No. 23 Squadron re-formed at Leeming with the Tornado F3, leaving the handful of F4s in the Falkland Islands to be known as 1435 Flight. Like the Gladiators protecting Malta in the Second World War, three of the aircraft soon became known as 'Faith', 'Hope' and 'Charity'. With typical black humour a fourth aircraft was nicknamed 'Desperation'.

Beautiful study of 56 Squadron's Diamond 9 formation. I was extremely grateful to OC 56 Barry Dogget and Tony Barmby for asking me to take these photographs. On a claggy East Anglian day we had to fly nearly 100 miles eastwards to find clear airspace over the North Sea.

The newly painted FGR2 XV472 flies over a snow-covered German landscape.

No. 19 Squadron's 'Charlie' was perhaps the RAF's dirtiest Phantom. It is seen here recovering to Italian Air Force base Decimomannu in Sardinia late in 1981.

The busy Cyprus flight line. No. 92 Squadron's T-bird has been partially repainted by 19's ever-busy groundcrew.

Back in the UK the Tornado F3 was rapidly being introduced to service after the three Leeming squadrons had formed. Leuchars gave up its long-serving FG1s; 111 Squadron formed with the F3 in 1990; and 43 Squadron decommissioned the Phantom in July 1989. Some thought had been given to selling on the retired FG1s but this proved to be a non-starter. Most of the airframes had already flown around 5,000 hours, and as no other air force operated the unique Spey-engined version they were duly scrapped. Most of the FG1s were scrapped at Leuchars but a few ventured south to Wattisham to join an ever-growing number of retired FGR2s. There were so many surplus FGR2s that the decision was taken in early 1991 to replace 74 Squadron's short-lived F4Js with freed-up FGR2s. The FGR2 commenced flying with 74 Squadron on 15 January 1991. The much-loved J model had seen just seven years' service. A big bonus for 74 Squadron converting to the FGR2 was that at last they had dual-control aircraft on strength. (The ex-US Navy F4Js had not included any dual-control variants.) All flying in trainers had previously had to be conducted in borrowed 56 Squadron aircraft. From a pilot's point of view the F4J was sadly missed as it offered better general handling characteristics, instant burner light-up and improved throttle response to name but a few of its advantages.

It was during this transition period that the Phantom should have undergone its biggest upgrade to date. Plans were afoot to give this ageing fighter a complete upgrade, including a single-piece front windscreen, digital INAS, upgraded RWR, improved avionics and various radar improvements. Sadly government cuts under the infamous Options for Change policy squashed all these plans and the only real development was the British Aerospace programme of building new outer wing panels. But the RAF Phantoms were to enjoy one final moment of glory. The Iraqi invasion of Kuwait in August 1990 left the British sovereign bases in Cyprus vulnerable to attack. The RAF's Tornado F3s were heavily committed to providing front-line cover in Saudi Arabia so the Phantoms were used to defend the island. Under the overall command of 92 Squadron, crews from both the units based in Germany spent over six months detached to this strategically important island. During their deployment there the crews provided excellent training for coalition forces transiting the area.

As the need for Phantom crews dwindled the OCU disbanded on 31 January 1991. Shortly afterwards the Tornado F3 took over the role of air defence for the Falkland Islands. The four FGR2s remaining in theatre never returned to the UK. Three were broken up on site but a fourth was preserved at Mount Pleasant. With the Wildenrath Wing about to be disbanded, Wattisham became the F4's last lair and 56 and 74 Squadrons were to be the last operators of this venerable beast. With only a handful of Phantom crews converting to type or retraining, 74 Squadron set up a small conversion cell within the squadron. As the last Phantom operators they also had the distinction of providing the last crew for the 1992 solo aerobatics season. In order to keep the 56 Squadron number plate alive the Tornado OCU adopted the Firebirds mantle. With a general easing of the rules 56 Squadron led the way in making its Phantoms more colourful, notably with shark's mouths and personalised codes. Eventually all the squadron's FGR2s had red tails. If not as glamorous as the chequerboard tails of the Lightnings, the FGR2s were still the most colourful Phantoms around. The squadron adopted the tail letters P H O E N I X F T R S and unit pride had never been stronger. The German squadrons, about to relinquish their own Phantoms, were not to be outdone. Two aircraft from 19 and 92 Squadrons were painted in an overall blue scheme while several others received blue and red fins. Just as RAF Binbrook had become the mecca for Lightning aficionados, so RAF Wattisham became the last resting-place for the Phantoms, and Phantom phanatics from

You can almost see the concentration on Lester Jackman's face as his Phantom slides up to the Victor tanker's left wing hose. Squadrons based in Germany were relative newcomers to the air-to-air refuelling game, only starting in the early 1980s.

Sunset Phantom, flown by Mick Mercer.

across the globe descended on the base to see the last of the Phantoms in action. Both Wattisham squadrons kept the image of the Phantom alive right to the bitter end, with 74 Squadron staging a mini Tiger Meet in September 1992, just weeks before they were due to re-equip with the diminutive Hawk trainer. As a centrepiece one grounded airframe (XV404) was painted in a stunning wrap-around Tiger scheme of black and orange. The intense rivalry between the two squadrons resulted in some notable achievements in these final days. During a detachment to RAF Akrotiri 56 Squadron managed to fly 56 sorties in one day. Not to be outdone, 74 Squadron put up 74 sorties – no mean feat with just 10 ageing fighters!

But the writing was on the wall and the venerable Phantom's days were numbered as a front-line fighter. Two decades previously Wattisham was the killing ground for the Lightning F Mk 3. Now, a mass cull of once-proud Phantoms was to take place within sight of 56 Squadron's dispersal, as FG1s and FGR2s fell in growing numbers to the cutter's torch. Despite the rapid run-down and premature demise of the mighty Phantom, they saved the best till last. With both squadrons remaining fully operational to the very end, the Suffolk skies were filled with some memorable sights in those final days: 74 Squadron put up a final Diamond 9 when the F4Js were replaced; five J models led a box of four FGR2s in the murky January mist; and in June 1991 56 Squadron put up several immaculate Diamond 9s. Not to be outdone, the then AOC Sir John Allison led a memorable formation of sixteen Phantoms using a mix of 56 and 74 Squadron machines. Originally planned to be four Box 4s, the Diamond 16 proved popular from Buckingham Palace to Boscombe Down in the summer of 1992.

In June 1992 56 Squadron finally gave up Phantom operations but 74 Squadron, the last Phantom operators, were operational quite literally to the end. They took part in Exercise ARC (an Anglo-French exercise) on 29–30 September – and stood down the following day.

Marked with blue crosses, the last Phantoms were towed outside and broken up on site. Fortunately a few were preserved for museums or to act as gate guards. However, as the RAF continued to shrink some of these survivors were also scrapped a short time later. The passing of the Phantom marked the end of an era, as for the first time in many years the Royal Air Force was left with a single fighter type, the Tornado F3. Although it never fired a missile in anger, the Phantom had served operationally throughout the world. Gone but never forgotten, the Phantom's passing ended another chapter in the RAF's glorious history.

CHAPTER 2

Andy's QRA Phantom

Andy Kirk

I completed three tours on the RAF Phantom: one on 43 Squadron, one on 19 Squadron and one on 228 OCU, teaching on the aircraft. One of the most exciting experiences was serving on the Quick Reaction Alert (Interception) Force, known as 'Q'. At RAF Leuchars both 43 and 111 Squadrons were tasked with Northern QRA, a NATO assignment which they took turns to fulfil with their FG1 Phantoms. No. 43 Squadron received the first RAF FG1 Phantoms soon after the Royal Navy's plan to fit out two aircraft carriers with the type ran short of funds.

On 'Q' at Leuchars, two crews and aircraft, together with their five groundcrew, manned a special building known as the 'Q' shed, where they waited in flying clothing, listening to the telebrief for urgent scramble orders; the crews had to be airborne within ten minutes of a scramble order from RAF Buchan. However, it was more usual to have quite a long period of notice, as Russian aircraft usually took off from the Kola peninsula and followed a route past northern Norway (where they would be intercepted by Norwegian F16s) and then south-westwards down the Norwegian Sea. The radar track would be handed over by Norwegian controllers to the UK, and crews at RAF Leuchars could often have as much as a couple of hours before taking off in good time to intercept the Russian aircraft as they penetrated the UK Flight Information Region to the east of Iceland. The Phantoms were specially modified for the task; they were fitted with eight missiles and three fuel tanks, and weighed in at nearly 60,000lb. An external power set was used to start the engines as the aircraft did not have an internal battery. In addition, telebrief was fitted to enable direct communication with RAF Buchan. For a no-notice scramble, the telebrief would suddenly proclaim 'Leuchars alert 2 Phantoms', followed by the message to the crews, now in their aircraft, 'Vector 350, climb angels 200, and call Buchan on Fighter Stud 60'. There was trouble for any crews who were airborne late, frequently resulting in additional doses on 'Q'. It was normal for the first aircraft to check in to be scrambled, whether or not it was the nominated Q1 aircraft, so there was always competition to check in first!

At the same time the Victor tankers from RAF Marham would also be alerted, although they were some thirty minutes further south. The first Phantom crew would usually intercept the Russians in the south Norwegian Sea area, but would soon run short of fuel and would have to

Air refuelling was normally taught on the squadrons so it was rare to see OCU aircraft on the wing. Taking on fuel from the Victor's wing hoses are a pair of 64 Squadron 'scarab beetle' FGR2s.

give way to the Q2 crew, who would arrive on task with the tanker. Nevertheless, the aircraft frequently covered large distances either searching for or accompanying Russian Bears and Mays. It was important to keep track of your position during these missions. Despite its sophistication in radar terms, the FG1 navigation fit was sparse, being orientated around an air position indicator (API) that was fed with the met man's estimate of wind speed; it was always wrong, and keeping the aircraft from drifting off to Timbuktoo demanded some concentrated effort.

In Germany the RAF manned 'Q' at RAF Wildenrath. The two units there, 19 and 92 Squadrons, each provided an aircraft that was installed into a hardened aircraft shelter (HAS) in the 19 Squadron dispersal at the western end of the airfield. Here, the readiness state was 5 minutes to airborne, although the basing of 'Q' at Wildenrath often meant that we were arriving on task later than we would like. The difficulty was that the Phantoms had considerably greater range than the Harriers, with the result that during the changeover from the Lightning to the Phantom the 'Q' base moved from Gutersloh to Wildenrath, thus allowing the Harriers at Gutersloh to be closer to the Inner German Border. This would be their theatre should the Russians attack, with the fighters protecting them from above and behind. These Phantoms were the FGR2 model, which was the original aircraft as ordered by the RAF; they were fitted with an internal battery for remote starting, and a navigation suite built around an inertial platform. On 'Q' the aircraft were cocked for a scramble as at RAF Leuchars, but in Germany they were fitted with eight missiles, two fuel tanks and the famed 20mm SU23/A Gatling gun as per their NATO declaration. Again the aircraft were very heavy, and the gun was very 'draggy', resulting in somewhat shorter missions. There was rarely any warning of a sortie; because their efforts to identify a radar contact took time, the radar site staff frequently left their decision to launch 'Q' later than we would have liked. The Wing Ops Centre staff would just hit the alarm buzzer, and the Phantom crews would run out, strap in and start engines while waiting for scramble information. It was not unknown for the RAF police to visit us during their patrols of the area, and they always brought with them their large Alsatians. On one occasion one attached itself to my leg during the run to the aircraft, and for a while it seemed I would have to fly the 'Q' mission sharing the cockpit with a large dog – but luckily it came to nothing.

The 'Q' missions in Germany were always testing. The crew had no warning, nor did they ever have any information on what their task was. Sometimes it was a practice, and we might have to intercept a 60 Squadron Pembroke less than 20 miles away with a heavy aircraft and 150 knots of overtake. Equally, it could be a real mission in cloud along the Inner German Border looking for a suspected intruder. On one occasion we intercepted a glider east of Gutersloh which had apparently violated the buffer corridor with East Germany. Imagine what went through the pilot's mind as his silent reverie was interrupted by a Phantom passing close by with gear and flaps down as the crew tried to slow down sufficiently to take photographs. This particular pilot was apparently fined many Deutschmarks for this offence and had his pilot's licence revoked. On another occasion we were scrambled for a practice intercept of some German F104s that were flying southwards across Germany at Mach 0.9 at high level. This was a tough target in a fully laden Phantom straight after take-off. However, we got in beside them and set about the photography process. I looked through the camera, and asked the pilot to move closer. This he did, until we were as close as we could go. I shot several pictures of the F104, which half-filled the viewfinder, and we prepared to leave for home. It then transpired that I had photographed the wrong aircraft; we had been in close formation with the leader, but I had photographed, using a telephoto lens, his wingman, a mile away!

Photographed off the Scottish coastline in the late 1980s, 111 Squadron's colourful FG1 XV574.

Right: Two scruffy F4s prepare to take on fuel from a pristine Victor.

Below: QRA and tanking went hand-in-hand. Here, framed by the refuelling probe, an FGR2 takes on gas from the Victor's wing.

Life was never dull at Wildenrath. Tacevals and Maxevals were the order of the day for a base on such a high state of readiness. Often the crews were called in at 4 a.m. to man aircraft and prepare for an evaluation. This was a serious business, with guards, gas masks and live intruders. Thankfully, the 'Q' shelters were exempt from these exercises, although the crews could normally expect a scramble early on in any exercise. During these generation exercises, the groundcrew always did an excellent job of loading the aircraft with missiles, preparing them for flight and at the same time fighting off intruders. With a cocked aircraft and crew and the three groundcrew awaiting the scramble message in their HAS, the best option was to bolt the doors from inside the shelter so that you were safe from interference by intruders and evaluators alike! As ever, the best place to be on an evaluation was in the air, and there were usually plenty of targets sent up to penetrate the low-level radar caps in Low Flying Areas 1 and 3 in Germany and in the Ardennes area in Belgium. Our targets included many NATO aircraft types; there were German Alpha Jets and F104s and Dutch and Belgian F16s and Mirages. RAF Harriers and Jaguars often targeted for us, and our mission was to intercept them. We used film of our radar to show that we had done so successfully, and the films would be checked on our return to base. After one evaluation the Jaguar force regarded us with new respect when one of them was inadvertently shot down for real by an over-zealous crew with a fully armed Phantom!

Last, but by no means least, there were 'Q' operations in the Falkland Islands. This was, of course, the principal role of the fighters there, so other flying tasks were limited by the need to keep aircraft serviceable for 'Q'. Nevertheless, there were always two F4s in their shelters on 10 minutes' readiness to fly. Although there were

Opposite: An FG1 of 111 Squadron pictured shortly before the type was withdrawn from service.

A brand-new Tornado from the short-lived 23 Squadron flying alongside a blue-tailed 19 Squadron FGR2. In terms of capability the original Tornado F3 was no great leap forward.

'Visidents' were still the bread-and-butter of UK Phantom squadrons. This view is typical of the final position used to identify an aircraft.

some practice events, there was not a great deal of 'live' tasking. The crews came from the UK and Germany squadrons on rotation, and they only stayed for four weeks, as there was no guarantee that flying currency requirements (a minimum of one day flight every twenty-eight days) could be maintained, especially during the winter. On one occasion the OCU was tasked with changing over the F4s at Mount Pleasant Airfield, an operation that was to be conducted in complete radio and electronic silence as part of a practice reinforcement. With crews pre-positioned at Ascension Island, the Phantoms and tankers set off from Leuchars to cover the 9,000 miles to the Falklands. The operation was generally successful, although we had some interesting moments. Sitting on the dispersal at Ascension in 35 degrees C wearing an immersion suit was quite stressful, but not as worrying as losing sight of the tanker for 15 minutes halfway between Ascension Island and Mount Pleasant. The prospect of a diversion to South America did not appeal to the anxious crew!

The Soviet Bear bomber, favourite target of the Leuchars wing.

Together with the radar stations at Alice and Byron Heights, QRA's main role was to demonstrate that the islands were firmly in the hands of UK forces, and to intercept the probing Argentinian Air Force Lockheed Electra whenever it came near the patrolled zone. We sometimes employed stealthy approach techniques with excellent results. The most important factor in the Falklands was the weather, which could change very quickly. One moment it would be bright sunshine and light winds; the next moment the airfield could disappear in a blizzard, with virtually no visibility and strong crosswinds. On more than one occasion the C-130 tanker was scrambled to refuel the airborne fighters to allow them to hang about until the weather cleared. Then the C-130 would recover, followed by the Phantoms, which would land using the approach end cable to avoid having to brake on a snowy runway. These were testing times.

Since the fall of the Berlin Wall in 1989, the volume of unknown traffic penetrating the UK Air Defence Region has fallen greatly. The task of countering intruders with fully armed fighters has now fallen to the Tornado F3. Nevertheless, the FG1, FGR2 and F4J Phantoms provided the backbone of UK air defence during much of the Cold War and in many complex and testing situations. The crews loved their aircraft dearly, and salute those responsible for purchasing such an accomplished and capable machine.

CHAPTER 3

Falkland Islands Defender

Guy Bancroft-Wilson

In 1983 the F4 crews in the UK and especially RAF Germany regarded their four-month detachment to the Falkland Islands with little favour, but in fact it rewarded us with some excellent flying and realistic training in totally unrestricted airspace. I arrived on 27 March 1983, the day British Summer Time and the South Atlantic winter began. After 11 hours in an RAF VC10 (in-flight entertainment had kindly been removed), with a 1-hour refuelling stop in Dakar, we spent 9 hours on the ground in Ascension. Then followed an uncomfortable 12½-hour journey on Para seats in a fully packed C-130. On arrival at RAF Stanley we were met by the outgoing Phandet crew, who had completed their four-month tour. Initially known simply as 'Phandet' (Phantom Detachment), it was to become 23 Squadron just a month later.

The aircrew accommodation left a lot to be desired, although the *Coastel* – a floating hotel – had recently arrived and was to be our home every other night for the next four months. The *Coastel* was actually quite civilised, with a well-frequented Officers' Mess bar and restaurant, and a bunk in each small room which we shared with a squadron member from the opposite shift. Alternate nights were spent on a 10-minute QRA shift, housed in three Portakabins next to the aircraft and temporary hangers. One Portakabin was the operations room and offices, one was a crew room and the other was used for sleeping. There were ten Phantom crews with a minimum of four crews on QRA duty. Four crews flew day-to-day missions and one acted as operations officers. This meant we worked about 36 hours on and 12 hours off, and had one day off in every ten. This wasn't as bad as it sounded as crews preferred to be at work rather than have days off as leisure activities were limited to say the least. On average Q1 (the primary alert aircraft) was scrambled once a month for a perceived, suspected or unidentified threat. Once a week it would be scrambled for practice missions.

Our role was Falkland Islands Air Defence. To help us achieve that, a Falkland Islands Protection Zone (FIPZ) was established for a distance of 200 miles around the islands. The FGR2 was an excellent aircraft for the role

A 19 Squadron FGR2 flies at low level in Norway over scenery very similar to that encountered in the Falklands.

Most of the Falklands flying involved low-altitude (ultra-low) intercepts.

REAR S
CLOSE
OPEN

because of its speed and capability as a weapons platform. All the Phantoms in the Falklands were armed with four Aim 9L Sidewinders, four Skyflash missiles and the SU23 cannon. The latter fired at a rate of 100 rounds a second and we carried 1,200 rounds of tracer, ball and HE bullets. There was also a small detachment of Harrier GR3s which were used for daylight air defence and ship defence operations.

The flying in the Falklands was outstanding. There were no towns to be avoided (except Port Stanley) and very few wires, masts or pylons. There were no airways, airfields, danger areas or village fêtes to be avoided. The only thing we had to watch out for were Her Majesty's ships, whose crews, understandably, were still a bit nervous at the sight of high-speed fighters tracking towards them at low level. One disadvantage to Falkland Islands flying was the unpredictable weather. Fog could roll in at a moment's notice, resulting in another use for the F4's high-speed dash during a weather recall. The weather made for some interesting Phantom operations. The temperature never rose above 10 degrees C or fell below minus 10 degrees, and horizontal snow was not

Opposite: 'Backseater' showing the later addition of the vision scope filling in the left quarter light. This made the already claustrophobic office even worse.

Like those of the Germany squadrons, Falklands Phantoms were gun-armed. This shark-mouthed cannon sits in the old QRA shelter at RAF Akrotiri.

XV472 (L) skims the waves on a low-level attack.

uncommon – and nor were 100mph winds. During my first week in theatre there was no flying at all owing to the atrocious weather conditions.

I flew approximately seventy hours during my three-and-a-half months in the Falklands, including thirty-five sorties. This included high and low practice intercepts, similar-type air combat and dissimilar air combat against the Harrier and, uniquely, the Hercules. Such sorties were always popular because of their demanding nature. Flying a heavy Phantom against a tight-turning slow aircraft like a Harrier or a Hercules required a certain amount of experience on the Phantom as well as a degree of determination and care. After about an hour we would generally need to refuel (air-to-air) with the Hercules. This could take place anywhere from 20,000 feet down to as low as 250 feet over the sea or land.

A Presence Run would often follow tanking. This was a high-level transit to the western edge of the FIPZ, to ensure the Argentinian mainland would pick us up on radar to remind them of our presence. A low-level return would follow. Often the Phantoms would be scrambled to intercept the inbound air bridge Hercules and then escort it to Port Stanley. As part of our anti-shipping and ship defence role, we would practise ship attacks for the benefit of the Royal Navy. We also performed air-to-ground or air-to-sea strafe, a skill not normally practised by the UK or Germany air defence squadrons. These strafe missions would take place over land on a rocky outcrop or against a splash target towed behind a ship. About 15 per cent of all the sorties were flown at night. This allowed us to practise night air refuelling and close formation flying using night vision equipment.

Only two F4s could fly at any one time owing to landing restrictions at Port Stanley airfield. After the war the runway had been lengthened to approximately 6,000 feet using metal matting. Although a Phantom could land and stop within that distance we were always heavy with a full war load and sufficient fuel to hold off for weather, airfield or aircraft problems. This meant that every F4 landing used the rotary hydraulic arrestor gear (RHAG). There were three on the runway, one 300 metres in, another in the centre in case the hook jumped over the first and the third in the over-run. F4 landings were arranged to be spaced by fifteen minutes, giving the fire crews plenty of time to reset the cable. Apart from the tedious journey to and from the South Atlantic, being part of a large detachment of F4s in the Falklands was exciting and excellent experience, but two months was certainly long enough!

CHAPTER 4

'J' Driver

John Bletcher

It was a great big, ugly, slab-sided monster with the intimidating physical presence of the bare-knuckle fighter. It had street credibility in spades, and wherever you took it the F4 was never treated with anything less than respect, even by the F15 Eagle drivers. Ageing, battle-scarred heavyweight that it was, the Phantom could still deliver a damaging punch. It was not a machine to underestimate.

The first time I came to fly one was at RAF Coningsby in 1986. I had spent weeks in ground school learning about the systems that made it work, and hours in the simulator practising failures of those same systems. My navigator and I had run countless practice radar intercepts on a rather old-fashioned clockwork rig. So on the morning of my first trip, I was as prepared as I was ever going to be. And hugely excited – and just a little bit anxious. Close-up the F4 seemed even bigger. To get on board required a short climb up a retractable boarding step. Then you scaled the side of the fuselage using hidden hand and footholds, which were covered by spring-loaded covers. You hoisted yourself over the side of the cockpit and on to the seat, and then sat down, your feet and shins disappearing down the tunnels under the forward panel towards the rudder pedals. The cockpit was a rather roomy place. I always imagined it had been designed with hefty, bull-necked United States Marine Corps pilots in mind. So at 5 feet 7 inches and 165lb, I was never going to be cramped. The view from the office was awesome. Ahead of you was the tiny glass front windshield and gunsight with a radar repeater just below it. The forward panel had a massive and very reassuring artificial horizon (actually an attitude direction indicator (ADI), because, owing to some rather clever mechanical arrangement, the horizon also worked like a compass in azimuth), a large horizontal situation indicator (HSI) slightly lower, and on either side an airspeed indicator and altimeter. The stick top protruded just above the knees, with buttons for nosewheel steering and weapons selection, and a large coolie-hat switch for trimming. On the left were two large man-sized throttles, with switches for radios. Forward on the left was the gear handle, a large sturdy lever with a large round bulb on the end of it. Forward on the right were the engine instruments, and further back the side-panel for the radios and transponder controls. Ergonomics was a relatively unknown science when the F4 was conceived, so switches, lights and various gauges were peppered around the cockpit, all tucked in where space was available, rather than being systematically positioned for operator convenience. Having said that, it wasn't long before the Phantom began to feel like home.

E
W

The RAF's J model Phantoms were unique in many ways. Delivered in a different shade of green they were normally flown with a centreline tank only. Here 'Whisky' and 'Echo' sit on the RAF Leeming flight line ready to start. The black umbilical is actually the air start equipment used to fire up the American J79 engines.

This J model is seen crossing the Wash, and looks as if new outer wing panels have been applied.

After the Hawk, which was a nimble little jet, the F4 felt like a Mack truck. It was after all designed to operate from carriers, and was built accordingly. Everything was big, tough and sturdy. But the biggest difference was in the performance. Sure enough the Hawk went round corners better than the Phantom did, but it could not match the fantastic rush that the two afterburning Speys delivered. My first take-off (with an extremely brave instructor sitting in the back seat to save me from myself) was unforgettable. The basic procedure was to line up on the runway, and hold the aircraft on the brakes. The throttles were gradually brought up towards the top end of the dry power range, then the engines were checked and the brakes released. As the aeroplane started to roll you pushed the thrust levers forward, allowed the engines to stabilise at maximum dry power, and then rocked the throttles outboard and advanced the engines into the reheat zone and WOW! . . . 25 tons of very solid aeroplane started to rush towards the horizon as though the very hounds of hell were chasing it. The stick was held back until the nosewheel lifted, and then a slight check forward maintained the attitude. There was nothing more to do now except keep a weather eye on the engine gauges and airspeed indicator, and just allow the aeroplane to fly itself. And there you were, airborne on two bright plumes of heat, fire and noise. Then it was time to get the wheels up, and then the flaps, and then wait for 300 knots or so, deselect the reheat and continue the climb, allowing the aeroplane to accelerate towards 350 knots. The first time I did this, I think the F4 had got to 20,000 feet by the time my brain had made it halfway down the runway. . . .

Barry Cross, an ex-Red Arrows pilot, holds top rudder to produce a pleasing camera angle.

A black-tailed J.

I always felt fairly secure in the Phantom. It had a fearsome reputation for punishing errors of handling, especially at low speed. Indeed I got my fingers burned very badly on one occasion, although I lived to tell the tale. But if you observed the rules and didn't take huge liberties, the Phantom would generally keep you out of trouble. It had a proven pedigree in Vietnam where the US forces had proved it strong enough to get the job done and tough enough to absorb some battle damage and still bring you home. There is a Norwegian Cessna 152 pilot who has every reason to thank whichever deity he holds dear that he led a good life. We were on detachment up in Rygge, and on this particular afternoon were working against some particularly determined F16 drivers. The F16 is a tiny aeroplane and extremely difficult to acquire visually head on, especially in poor visibility. It was not a pleasant day to be operating at low level. The terrain was hilly, making the radar handling hard going for the navigators. The weather was less than ideal, grey and murky, and the cloudbase was down about the 2,500 foot mark. Added to all this, we were working in free airspace – which meant we were sharing the area with civilian light aircraft going quietly about their business.

We were prosecuting an attack against an F16 which my Nav. had picked up on radar. I was working extremely hard to pick up this guy visually, with limited success. The range was coming down fast and I was starting to think that blowing through the merge was the sensible option on this run when I noticed something just on the nose of the aircraft. The view ahead in the

A mass of rivets. This F4J seems to have had its radome repainted. The crews are wearing standard RAF helmets, indicating that this was late on in the J's service.

An electrician (known in RAF slang as a 'fairy') works hard to fix this J model radar. In the background an unmarked Tornado taxies out for an evening mission. The shot was taken at Leeming during the build-up to the Gulf War (August 1990). F4Js were deployed to Leeming to act as Iraqi Floggers to test the Tornado F3s.

F4 is hampered by the metalwork and brackets supporting the gunsight and angle of attack gauge, and by the chunky canopy arch. These drastically reduce visibility through the front screen, so it is not unusual to have an aircraft directly ahead obscured by these mountings. Sure enough, from behind the left-hand side of the canopy arch emerged a small aircraft. At times like this, events seem to slow down. As I write this, I can recall with perfect clarity the cold realisation that we were running up behind a small light aircraft. We were travelling at 400 knots in several tons of serious aeroplane. He was tootling along at 90 knots in something that might as well be built out of Baco-foil for all the good it would do him in a collision. And there was no doubt in my mind that we were close enough to do him some serious damage. Fractionally later I realised that it was a high-wing monoplane, a Cessna 150 or something similar. While this was going on I rammed the throttles forward into full reheat and heaved back on the stick. Once I got the nose of the Phantom up and away from the Cessna, I checked the pitch and rolled left, holding the F4 on its wingtip and searching frantically for the light aircraft we had most likely swatted out of the sky. Not a sign. I explained to the back-seater what was going on and we flew a couple of lazy orbits left and right to see if we could spot the unfortunate Cessna. There was no sign of him anywhere, and no transmissions on the guard frequency either. I wasn't totally reassured by any of this, and on our return to the base, I went to find one of the Norwegians. I explained what had happened, and asked if there had been any reports of overdue civilian aircraft. He was quite relaxed about the whole thing and told me that things like this happened all the time in Norway. I was still somewhat dubious about the whole issue, but the next two days passed uneventfully and I began to think that maybe the Cessna pilot did not notice us as we narrowly avoided making an early appointment for him with his maker. As if! The

ZE359 J. Fuji Velvia is the preferred film for air-to-air photography. It is superb for producing deep saturated colours accentuating the light at altitude.

next day I was lounging in the crew room when one of the Norwegians popped his head round the door to ask if it was me who nearly ran over a light aircraft earlier in the week. I nodded warily. 'OK', the Norwegian said brightly, 'well, the pilot of the Cessna is on the phone and wants to talk to you.'

Talk to me? If it were me, I would want to do something more than talk! Anyway I headed off to the Ops room and picked up the phone. Much to my surprise, there was a remarkably chipper individual on the other end. I did my bit for Anglo-Norwegian relations and apologised profusely for the whole event. He was remarkably sanguine about the whole thing, so I asked him what he saw from his aeroplane.

'Well,' he said, 'I was just flying along minding my own business when I heard a very loud roar, my aeroplane rocked about a bit [here I began to suspect some classic Scandinavian understatement] and then right ahead of me I saw two really bright orange lights which vanished ahead.'

'What did you do then?' I asked.

'Oh, I went home, landed and had a drink,' he said.

'How close do you think we were?' I asked.

'Oh, quite close, I think.' More understatement.

Mr Norwegian, you have no idea!

CHAPTER 5

Battle Flight Scramble

Ian Black

The banshee wail of the alert siren wakes us from our patchy sleep. The morning songbirds are just starting their dawn chorus. We've been on duty for over twenty hours. Like me, my pilot is fatigued from a restless day. Without thought we leap from our beds semi-clothed, trailing the paraphernalia of the jet jockey's wardrobe behind us. Like startled rabbits we scramble to our warren. Twenty paces away our man-made metal war-horse, a Phantom, lies dormant. Awaiting its crew it stands sentinel in the morning sunrise.

The drive from my single postwar accommodation takes about 10 minutes. I've dined in style in the Officers' Mess, waited on hand and foot by tentative local staff. As I leave the domestic area my world, already drab, turns a darker shade of olive green. I pass row after row of low, industrial-style buildings all one colour. Each is hidden among dense pines. As my view opens up I pass rows of menacing Bloodhound missiles, all facing east and poised to counter the threat of the Warsaw Pact. Built in the early 1960s, these Thunderbird 1-like missiles have lost their shiny white paint. Now, like everything else on this war station, they have been 'toned down'. The world is olive drab. The surveillance radar mounted high on the bunker prescribes a lazy arc, scanning constantly for the unusual. Even the daily civilian troop carrier is scrutinised for hostile intent. I am now entering the real world. Far removed from my domestic bliss I'm driving into the Cold War zone. Unlike my UK counterparts, we are the tip of the sword, the cutting edge of RAF Germany's air defence plan. The traffic lights are fixed on bright green as I cross the threshold of runway 27. From here I can see our squadron complex – concrete scabs dotted among the Germanic woodland. Giant concrete shelters have superseded the revetments of the 1950s. Each houses two McDonnell Douglas Phantoms, the RAF's most potent warplane. Nuclear strike, battlefield interdiction, armed recce or air defence: no role is beyond its grasp. These are war-planes in every sense of the word. Bristling with all the delights of modern aerial warfare, they are machines of high repute. We are in the same mould as our carefree heroes, the crews who fought before us with such distinction. But we are only actors in this phoney war. We don't play active roles; we train and wait, hoping that our scene will never happen. If we do take the Phantom into combat, it will be

Night view of Germany's Battle Flight shelter, photographed in 1981. Surrounded by the paraphernalia required to keep a Phantom operational, the crew pose for a picture.

under very different rules. We may not even see our enemy, for we can shoot beyond visual range. We may have to operate under attack from nuclear weapons or, worse, chemical/biological weapons. For us there will be no cricket next to our parked Spitfires and Hurricanes. We will be entombed in our blast-proof shelters until the war is over.

I stop thinking and park my car among the rapidly filling spaces; I have my own slot. These are normally reserved for senior officers or administrators but 'Battle Flight Crew' is painted in blue in an otherwise green sea. It's nearly 8 a.m. and I've just enough time to collect all my chattels – bone dome, life jacket, anti-G suit, gloves, paperwork – there's always paperwork. As I look ahead only one building is not made from concrete. The flying clothing section is a prefabricated Portakabin marked for 'peacetime use only'. Inside the first thing that hits me is the smell: a mix of rubber, sweat and grease. Inside the thirty or so lockers are kept the personal worlds of every pilot and navigator on the squadron, our names crudely marked on the doors in chinagraph pencil. Stickers and zaps adorn the lockers of seasoned crews, and previous fighter squadron mementoes are stuck to the metal casing. Most have been defaced with graffiti. Loyalty to 19(F) Squadron is fierce; *no one* is better than us. I open the locker door and examine my world. My anti-G suit has been hung up by the flying clothing workers from the previous day. They do a thankless but vital job, cleaning and servicing our flying equipment with monotonous regularity. I lift my speed jeans off the peg. They weigh a ton. Every pocket is crammed with useful gadgets. In the two bottom leg pockets I have my go-anywhere maps, terminal approach plates, en route supplement and Noddy guide. My go-anywhere maps are the result of a conversation with a super-steely Harrier mate from nearby Gutersloh. He explains to me over a beer that because the Jump Jet's cockpit is so small he's invented the ultimate map. He takes a low-flying chart, which measures about 16 square feet, then he covers it in Fablon and places the whole map in the bath to soak for twenty-four hours. Then he peels the white paper off the back leaving the coloured chart firmly stuck to the Fablon. This gives you a 16 square foot map, covering all of Northern Germany, that can be folded into the size of a handkerchief. After many failed attempts I now have said German hanky, albeit with a few areas of no-man's-land where I accidentally pulled the map off with the backing.

The American-style terminal approach plates allow me to talk my pilot through any instrument approach in Europe; it's a bulky tome. The en route supplement is the RAF Bible for aircrews. It has every conceivable piece of information needed to operate in European airspace. It's definitely a no-go item – meaning if you don't have one you don't fly. My green plastic Noddy guide is simply a wallet filled with plastic pages, which I fill with useful trivia such as radio frequencies, aircraft serviceability codes, national identity markings and so on. I also carry a copy of the aircrew turn-round guide. This allows me to refuel and service the Phantom to a basic standard should we divert to a non-Phantom base. More importantly, it tells me how to make the aircraft safe should we divert from Battle Flight with a live-armed aircraft. Pins inserted into the Sparrow/Skyflash missiles render them harmless, and the process is similar for the gun and the Sidewinders.

I have two knee pockets above my leg-restraining garters. Inside the left pocket is the Phantom FGR2 emergency checklist, coloured

Dropping towards low level over the River Rhine.

red for obvious reasons. In bold letters across the covers it says 'Check Circuit Breakers'. In the back cockpit on the right-hand side is a bank of hundreds of circuit breakers. More often than not, resetting the relevant circuit breaker can rectify a fault. For this purpose all Phantom navigators carry a purpose-made tool about the size of a large metal pencil with a forked end. This can be slid down the side of the ejector seat to pull and reset awkward CBs. In my right knee pocket I carry a copy of the Phantom Normal checklist. This has all the pre-take-off and landing checks. Additionally it carries in abridged form performance data for best range and cruise performance.

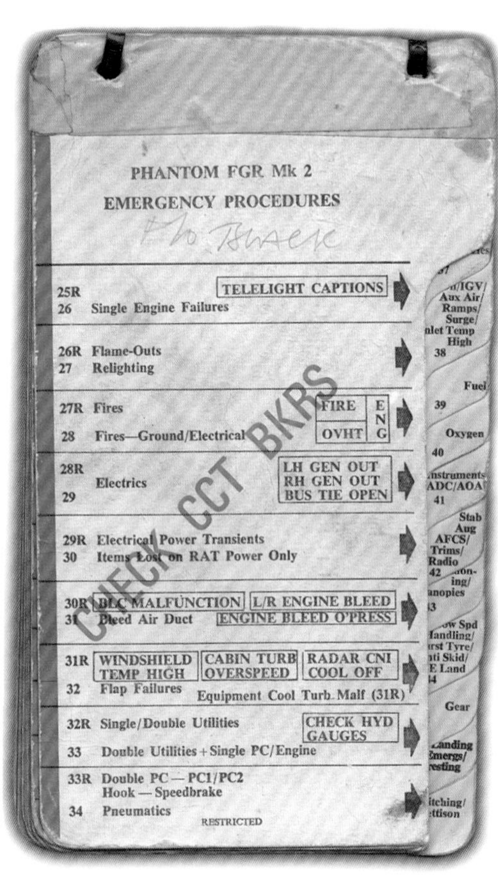
PHANTOM FGR Mk 2
EMERGENCY PROCEDURES
25R TELELIGHT CAPTIONS
26 Single Engine Failures
26R Flame-Outs
27 Relighting
27R Fires FIRE ENG OVHT
28 Fires—Ground/Electrical
28R Electrics LH GEN OUT RH GEN OUT BUS TIE OPEN
29
29R Electrical Power Transients
30 Items Lost on RAT Power Only
30R BLC MALFUNCTION L/R ENGINE BLEED
31 Bleed Air Duct ENGINE BLEED O'PRESS
31R WINDSHIELD TEMP HIGH CABIN TURB OVERSPEED RADAR CNI COOL OFF
32 Flap Failures Equipment Cool Turb. Malf (31R)
32R Single/Double Utilities CHECK HYD GAUGES
33 Double Utilities + Single PC/Engine
33R Double PC — PC1/PC2
Hook — Speedbrake
34 Pneumatics
RESTRICTED
CHECK CCT BKRS

On my right thigh, sewn into the nylon material, is a knife patch containing an aircrew knife and sheath. The knife is cunningly attached to the G-suit with a tie fastener so that if it comes loose from its sheath it won't drift around the cockpit and become a loose article hazard. The knife's main purpose is to deflate the dinghy mounted under my seat if it inflates in flight, although most guys use it to sharpen chinagraph pencils or open beer bottles. On top of my knee pockets are two clear Perspex pads. These I use to note all the details pertinent to that flight, such as call sign, weather, tactics leader, deputy leader frequencies and so on. Normally people use white pads with black or blue crayons. Now, with the tone-down in full force, the steely ones have green pads and yellow crayons. A flash of white kneepad might be all your adversary sees. At the top of my G-suit is a long rubber tube. This is connected to the ejector seat and pumps air into my speed jeans when we pull G. The theory is that as you pull G the blood rushes from the head to the feet. This forces you to lose consciousness. The G-suit counters this by inflating with air, crushing your legs and thus forcing the blood back to the brain. Tests show that it gives you an extra 1 or 2 G tolerance in combat.

I sling my G-suit over my left shoulder and pick up the next heavy item, the life preserver. Not quite up to auto-inflating standards yet, the life preserver is once again green outside but it turns Day-Glo orange once inflated. The life jacket really is what it says it is – a life preserver. Made by Beaufort in Liverpool, they have saved many a crew from the cold North Sea. A beaded handle inflates the stole in a matter of seconds. In the two side pockets are emergency radio distress flares and a heliograph. As our role is overland low-level air defence we take little interest in sea survival. We are all of the opinion that it really wouldn't be your lucky day if you ejected into a lake in the middle of Germany in winter. We all fly in summer attire pretty much all year. If it's really cold we wear a cold weather flying jacket but that's about it. With my outer garments complete I close the metal door and collect my Mk 3 bone dome from its wooden locker. Like a well-worn glove after hours of use it's a perfect fit but it's showing its age and is covered with dents and scrapes. Fortunately the flying clothing workers known as 'squippers' (safety equipment workers in full) clean my visor and mask daily removing all the grime and sweat that accumulates after each mission. Armed with all I need I collect my paperwork and take the short walk to the Battle Flight shelter. It stands alone close to the runway threshold, nestling among the trees. The door to the crew accommodation is already ajar. The off-going crew are impatient to get away. A day off is given after twenty-four hours' continuous duty. We shake hands. They look bleary-eyed after a night in the shed. My

All-weather ops meant exactly that! As part of the border policing control the Germany Phantoms were on constant alert 24 hours a day 365 days a year. This meant that no matter how bad the weather the crews had to be able to launch and intercept any target. Here XV497 taxies out for a low-level patrol during the cold winter of 1982.

pilot is already there, signing the authorisation sheets. They contain very little information: just the aircraft (Phantom FGR2 XV497), our crew names and 'Battle Flight duties as required'. Normally every minute detail is covered in the authorisation log: minimum heights, maximum speeds, evasion limits and so on. But today's mission is unknown. While the pilot signs for the aircraft and examines the technical log, I talk with the off-going navigator about the state of the rear cockpit. He gives me an idea how the INAS is performing and hands over the secret Noddy guide. The INAS is the inertial navigation and attack system – the Phantom's brain. Apart from telling us where we are it also feeds the pilot his attitude information; again, if it doesn't work it's a no-go item. If the INAS fails we stay firmly on the ground. Inside the secret Noddy guide is a plethora of facts: secret frequencies to contact our ground-based controllers, mission profiles and a host of codewords. We know that just outside the perimeter fence Soviet agents watch our every move. Binoculars are trained on us twenty-four hours a day and satellites pass overhead recording us like tiny ants. We are all vigilant about security.

In the back of the book are missile firing profiles. About once a year Battle Flight will be given a no-notice scramble to head west not east. Its target for the mission is a small drone in Cardigan Bay off the Welsh coast, at which one of the underslung missiles is fired. This is the ultimate test of all the equipment. After the missile launch the aircraft will have insufficient fuel to return to Germany and instead makes a lunch stop at RAF Valley. It also offers the crew a chance to get the morning's papers and any other items unobtainable in Germany. For us the chances of flying west are remote. England is fogbound from London to Yorkshire. If we go at all, our mission will be east.

The off-going crew depart and we saunter next door to chat with the groundcrew. Unlike us they spend a week at a time in this two-star prison. For us it's generally three days a month.

Night scrambles were rare though not uncommon. Burners blazing, XV496 blasts into the winter sky.

Thursdays are treasured duties as they give you a long weekend. Saturdays are least popular. In all, during a three-year tour most crews will spend over three months on duty in the Battle Flight shed. We talk carefully with the groundcrew about our individual responsibilities. If we are to get this beast airborne in five minutes it's going to require a lot of teamwork and coordination. Everyone needs to know who's going to do what if the hooter blows. The first hour on alert is all about checks. We have a land-line in the aircrew sitting room which is connected both to wing operations and sector control. We call them both to check they can hear us and vice versa. Once a week wing operations has a Battle Flight doors check. When they press the big red button deep in their concrete bunker 2 miles away the doors to the shelter open automatically. Everyone on duty needs to know when the test is to be done or all hell breaks loose. Of course, jolly japes are often the order of the day among fighter crews. As soon as one of the crewmen falls asleep during the day it's great sport to surreptitiously call wing ops and ask for a test of the Battle Flight doors. Watching your crewmember leap from his chair like a headless chicken as the klaxon goes off provides huge entertainment and lightens the boredom. As the hooter sounds the two giant metal clamshell doors glide open to reveal the Phantom's lair. From outside the jet certainly looks the part. Never was there (nor will there ever be) such a mean-looking jet war-plane. The yanks called it 'Double Ugly' or the 'Rhino'. The Brits more conservatively just call it the F4. With its up-turned wings and down-turned stabilator this is one mean machine. Bristling with weapons, the Phantom fully tooled up is an awesome sight. Strapped under its slab belly is the SU23 Gatling

Standard fit for 2ATAF Phantoms included centreline gun, two fuel tanks and a full complement of Sparrow/Skyflash missiles, as well as four AIM 9G/L heat-seeking missiles. For training this F4 carries a pair of forward ballast Sparrows and no Sidewinders.

gun capable of firing 1,234 rounds a minute. It could ruin Ivan's whole day with one HE round. The aircraft is in the standard 2ATAF war fit: gun, four AIM 9G Sidewinders (rear aspect heat-seekers) and four AIM 7 Sparrows. This was before all-aspect AIM 9Ls and Skyflash. We don't even have self-defence chaff and flares. The Phantom's reputation is legendary, the plane earning its battle spurs in the Vietnam War, taking out MiG fighters in the air-to-air role then diving down to pound enemy ground positions. In that conflict the versatile Phantom mastered every mission to which it was assigned.

Under the left wing a long thick black vein attaches itself, anaconda-like, to the underbelly. The electrical feed from the Houchin ground power unit will breathe life into this dormant monster should we be scrambled. Independently my pilot and I walk around the aircraft. An instructor of mine once said to me, after I'd taken an age inspecting the aircraft, 'You're flying it, not buying it!' I ignore such remarks. With only 5 minutes to be airborne there will be no second chance. No time to take a safety pin from a missile, no chance to stop to check for leaks or loose panels. Once we're in the cockpit we're going, save for a red warning light. While my pilot sets up the front office to his liking I climb the ladder to the back seat. It's about 10 feet up – and from the top of the ladder the first impression one gets is that the back seat is like a sunken coal-hole. The fuselage rises up around you as you sink into the seat. The groundcrew connect the external power and I select the INAS to Standby. Already warm, it relies on electrical power to heat the oil bath that the gyros sit in. If we scramble I'll give it a rapid alignment. This will be good enough for our needs but the accuracy of the navigational computer will be poor. As time is not a factor I run a full alignment, which will take a little over ten minutes. All the time I'm conscious that should we be scrambled now I'll still be able to flick the switch and make our five minutes. While the INAS aligns itself I check that the radio works and that all the radar switches are in the correct eye-pleasing position. I also have time to give the ejector seat a thorough check, making sure all the relevant safety pins are fitted inside the shelter. I carefully lay the shoulder straps on the side of the cockpit ready for the groundcrew to fasten me in. Once the INAS check is complete I dismount, happy in the knowledge that I can get the rear seat fired up in a couple of minutes. Squadron pride hangs in the balance here, for across the tarmac the crew from our sister squadron are performing their checks on the other Battle Flight Phantom. Normally whoever checks in first gets launched. It's decidedly uncool to be second. As we close the hangar door and walk back to the shed the clock strikes at 9.30 – just 23 hours to go! Now all we have to do is sit and wait.

Most crews leave their helmets and life jackets at the bottom of the aircraft ladder, but wherever you leave them you need to know where they are without thought. To be unable to get airborne in a no-notice scramble because you can't find your helmet would be disastrous.

As the day-to-day operations of the squadron come to life elsewhere on the airfield, the two crews of Battle Flight sit out the day poised like coiled springs waiting for the off. Squadron mates trundle past our accommodation in sedate un-armed jets, but at least we have the satisfaction of knowing our aircraft are live-armed. Wave after wave, they taxi past during the day, each crew in turn glancing at the less fortunate men stuck in the shed. Throughout the day most crews catch up on the obligatory

Both 19 and 92 Squadrons held an aircraft on five minutes' readiness. If one squadron was deployed it fell to the remaining squadron to provide both aircraft and spares. This was a huge drain on resources and curtailed the flying programme significantly.

Occasionally the Wildenrath wing would swap aircraft. Here a drab 19 Squadron FGR2 leads a brightly coloured 92 Squadron FGR2. XV411 was a long-serving 19 Squadron jet, having previously served the squadron as (M). The painted tails, long out of fashion, were the result of a series of mid-air collisions and were intended to make the aircraft more conspicuous at low level.

paperwork, filling in logbooks, statistics, travel claims, leave forms – the list is endless. Periods of administrative tedium are broken by the need to eat. The highlight of the day is phoning the all-ranks' mess to see what the day's menu is. It seems that unlike the wartime pilots who got the best of rations we are definitely at the bottom of the pile. Our ready-made meals are brought by Landrover in 'Hot locks' – pre-heated tin canisters. A typical meal is chicken in gravy followed by chocolate pudding – trying to work out which is which is the hardest task of the day! All too often it is looked at, pushed around the plate and quickly consigned to the bin. Luckily we do have a kitchen and 'dry rations' so we can at least attempt to cook for ourselves.

After lunch, it's either siesta time or we plod diligently through one of the many classified books held in the safe. If I want to know the instantaneous turn performance of a MiG 23 armed with two Atoll missiles and a gun or the max G available to said MiG pilot at 5,000 feet and 420 knots I just have to look in the safe. I could spend hours poring over energy graphs, radar signatures and other highly classified details. We also have pictures to look at: books full of grainy shots of the Soviet Union's most classified fighters fill the safe. I sit wondering how these fuzzy images of Floggers, Fishbeds and Fitters came to be in the West's hands. No doubt some very brave chap sat in a tent somewhere in East Germany trying to conceal his Nikon while snapping away. Somehow the fuzzy black and white images make the enemy aircraft look more menacing and they acquire a certain mystique that fills me with respect for their machines. I flick through the pages nonchalantly, skipping the reams of helicopter pictures but staring intently at

A variety of tails on the Wildenrath wing. Phantoms: some with grey tails and some camouflaged, and some with RWR and some without.

the fighter-bombers. All of them bear a striking resemblance to western fighters. The Flogger is a dead ringer for the Jaguar, the Fencer looks like a copy of the F-111 and the venerable Fitter could easily pass for the English Electric Lightning. If the balloon goes up and we have to face the might of the Warsaw Pact for real, there'll be little or no time for recce lessons. My pilot and I might have just 3 or 4 seconds to decide whether an oncoming aircraft is friendly or hostile, and there is no margin for error. As my blink rate decreases I realise it's time for a break. Wandering outside I look at my surroundings, encased in First World War-style barbed wire. Life seems tense. Perhaps that's why the Germany squadrons play as hard as they work. The crews live with the constant threat of conflict . . . all-out nuclear war. The reality doesn't bear thinking about. Our sister bases at Bruggen and Laarbruch also have aircraft on alert. But theirs is a different mission. Very different. Each armed with a single nuclear warhead, their Jaguars and Buccaneers won't be policing the skies like us. Their task is very much more serious: a one-way strike mission armed with something much more deadly than a Sidewinder.

By late afternoon my pilot and I, bored with the tedium, play cards; losing badly I admit defeat; perhaps I don't have the mental aptitude for snap. I decide to stretch my legs. I wander past the

groundcrew lounge towards the kitchens. Every few hours our groundcrew check our Phantom. Like doctors whose patient is on life support, they fuss over our baby, checking for leaks. Tell-tale pools of fluid oozing from its belly will put us 'off state'. If this happens the squadron has to get the Battle Flight spare in quickly to replace our sick jet; fortunately this is a rare event. As the evening draws in activity around the squadron dies down until all the aircraft are back, all safely accounted for. Having watched the obligatory video I ring our sister squadron crew, located 25 yards from us. We arrange to meet midway to swap videos. As a precaution I don my anti-G suit and stroll towards the 92 Squadron shelter. I see Keith, my opposite number, walking towards me. He looks at me intently. Perhaps he's realised that I'm more clothed than he is. He knows that if the hooter goes I'm going to check in first. We meet midway and exchange pleasantries. Like soldiers from the First World War we have left our lines to meet in no-man's-land: the divide between 19 and 92. We chat aimlessly and then bid our farewells. We watch their film. The night passes slowly and we retire to bed. Keeping as few clothes on as possible we climb into our beds, hoping not to be disturbed.

At nearly 7 a.m. we are in a deep slumber. Our telebrief crackles as sector operations try to talk to us; it falls on deaf ears. Semi-awake I hear a loud wail and my brain tells me this is definitely not an alarm clock. It seems like an age before I realise I'm not in my normal bed and this is not my wake-up call. Rapidly I roll to the left and start to gather speed towards the door. My pilot is two steps behind me. There's no time to converse, but we know what we have to do. At the bottom of the aircraft ladder I grab my life preserver and don it as fast as I can. My pilot is ahead of me, already halfway up the ladder. Wrapping my G-suit around my lower half I hear the reassuring cough of our ground power unit bursting into life. I leap up the ladder like a rat out of an aqueduct. Plugging my personal connector into the seat I pull my bone dome on to my head and plug my microphone into its socket. Instinctively my right foot presses the floor switch and I transmit: 'Mike Lima 51 cockpit ready.' I can hear my heart pounding through my flying suit; a heady mixture of adrenalin, fear and excitement fills my body. I wait, silently praying we've beaten our sister squadron to the check-in. We have. 'Mike Lima 51, this is Backwash, vector 070 climb angels 15, call TAD 473. SCRAMBLE – SCRAMBLE – SCRAMBLE, "acknowledge".' In an organised panic a flurry of fingers sets the Phantom's brain into gear as I align the INAS. My pilot is going about his business, the straps criss-crossing his life preserver attaching him to the Martin Baker marvel. As I perform the same drills my right eye catches the slow methodical red pulse of my INAS light. This tells me the gyros are spinning up and all for the moment is hunky dory. I listen in envy as my driver starts the left engine: engine master on, engine start switch to start check for rotation and move the left throttle through the gate to idle. I've been through it in my head so often hoping one day that I can follow suit. I'd never admit it but being a pilot is the ultimate kick – maybe one day. His eyes busily scan a multitude of dials called RPM, TGT, FIRE, OVHT, PC1 and so on – meaningless letters to the uneducated but mind-sharpeners to the steely fighter pilot. Checking the left engine has brought life to this dormant beast my pilot can now signal the groundcrew to disconnect external power; the life support is no longer needed. The left engine can happily run the Phantom, and now it will start the right Spey. Now our partnership must come together. When my driver is ready to taxi I must have the inertial system fully aligned and in 'navigate'. If we move forward before it's ready the gyros are uncaged and the whole procedure must be restarted after a lengthy delay; our scramble would quickly be poached. The steady glow of the align light is my queue to go to 'navigate' and call for taxi. My pilot nudges the throttles and the Phantom moves slowly forward. A deft dab of brake and we exit our concrete shelter, checking left and right, and glide into the early morning summer sun. I run through an abbreviated pre-take-off checklist. To each challenge the pilot responds. 'Steps' – 'Up'; 'Oxygen' – 'contents Connection flow' – the list is long, twenty-four items to be exact. But all must be covered. As we approach the runway I do a last-chance silent check in my head – Canopy (down, locked, caption out), Controls (full and free movement checked), Captions (all extinguished), Pins (seven stowed) and lastly Wings (spread and locked). As I look over at the left and right outer wing sections I see that both tell-tale pins are down. If the wings were unlocked there would be an orange pin protruding. All these safety checks are the result of someone's misfortune.

A few years back an RAF Phantom lifted off from RAF Bruggen and both wings folded, as the outer wings had been left unlocked and, vitally, were not checked. I chop to frequency and call for take-off. We're cleared to take off from runway 27 with the wind 270 at 10 knots down the strip – ideal. A cursory glance to the right checks the approach is clear, although who else would be flying at this ungodly time heaven knows. As we line up my pilot advances the throttles fully forward to max military power and then pushes them through the gate into reheat. The acceleration isn't earth-shattering in a fully tooled-up jet, laden with Sidewinders, gun, fuel tanks and Sparrows. It's going to use a fair bit of concrete to get this beast airborne. I call the odd speed as we accelerate to the point of no return. As the nosewheel lifts off my pilot checks forward on the stick to avoid a tail scrape. Soon the Phantom is airborne. More checks – gear up, lights out, flaps up, warning lights out, fuel transfer as required – then I change frequency and tell the Wildenrath departure controller our intentions.

With a live scramble other aircraft move out of the way for us so we have no worries about conflicting traffic. As soon as we are airborne my pilot racks on the bank and reefs the heavy machine round the corner. We head east in search of our unknown quarry. As the mighty Phantom starts its turn I lean forward to grab the radar. With the G piling on I need all my strength to pull it from its stowed position up into my lap. I select radar on and wait for the time out. As with the indispensable INAS, without our radar we are a poor fighting machine. The radar is our eyes, probing far ahead into the sky, searching for targets. The electronic blips it produces are our raison d'être. The small black screen glows an eerie green as the scanner starts to sweep. My pilot has a repeater in the front but just as I can't fly the Phantom he can't operate the radar. Each of us knows our part and respects each other's abilities.

With the burner cancelled to save fuel, we climb at a steep angle searching for clearer blue air. Quickly we are passed to Clutch Radar, our middle airspace controller. Immediately he tells us to level at 15,000 feet and vector 070. In between calls my pilot and I automatically challenge each other on fuel status, weapon selections and position. Strangely we're heading towards the border but not directly. A north-easterly track will take us towards RAF Gutersloh, the RAF's most easterly German base and home of the Harrier. It was once an air defence station but in these Cold War days it's deemed more tactical to put the short-range jump jets near their intended

Night missions were a regular part of Phantom operations. Dated by the Volvo car in the background, this 1980s image sees a crew rushing through their pre-start checks prior to a dusk sortie.

For training purposes Battle Flight aircraft would be given a no-notice scramble to intercept an unknown target. Here Battle Flight escorts a fellow squadron aircraft back to home base.

targets. I make a mental note of our position; there's no time to look at a map. I select the Tacan to Gutersloh's frequency. Heading north-east at 9 miles a minute we're soon passed on to Backwash, our GCI. We're told to change to TAD 473. Now begins the navigator's one-armed paperhanger role. Reaching for my green book I look at the frequency which corresponds to TAD 473; secrecy is the key. As I dial up the allocated frequency I can be sure some Soviet agent somewhere is doing the same, either with a frequency scanner trying to find us or more than likely from his own codebook. I check in to Backwash. His accent is strong and his English succinct: 'Mike Lima 51 vector 050.' 'Roger 050, identify Alpha Delta', I reply. In order to authenticate his orders I need to be sure who he is. We both have identical codebooks and I need to make sure he responds with 'Papa', my code, which goes with Alpha Delta. I can almost hear the flurry of paper flying round the control room as he tries to quickly return the correct response. 'Papa.' We all breathe a sigh of relief. 'Mike Lima 51, your target low bearing 040 degrees 60 miles.' I reach into my knee pocket and pull out my go-anywhere map for Northern Germany. Simultaneously I select the radar to pulse Doppler mode. If the target is low ordinary pulse mode will be useless. In pulse Doppler the Westinghouse AWG 12 will see velocity only, which will give us a clue to our prey's position. The display is hard to interpret, indeed for the untrained eye it is impossible. Six months on the OCU gives each navigator the basics for operating this steam-driven contraption. In the beginning the radar was in a league of its own. Notoriously unreliable, it was nevertheless the best around. Constant updates kept it viable, as digital boards replaced valves and reliability was improved. Still in the mid-1980s we reign supreme as our radar has the longest range and the best low-level detection ability. With so much going on I flick a few switches and the radar is now in automatic mode. It scans a vast space of sky and will give me an automatic range to any target it sees. I can now devote more of my time to navigating, helping my pilot with his situational awareness. If we need to descend to low altitude we need to be sure we know our position to within a few yards.

Closing the throttles my pilot lowers the nose and we soon point groundwards. Vast swathes of medium cloud engulf the jet as we hit our descent speed. My head is full of facts and figures: safety altitude, QNH and position. I check and recheck our on-board computer, the INAS. Reluctant to rely on that entirely I select the Tacan to a local beacon. All looks good and I'm happy where we are. I flick the radar back to pulse mode to map the ground ahead. There is a big town ahead, which corresponds to our calculated position. Shining brightly on the scope like a beacon, it reassures me that we aren't about to become another Flight Safety statistic.

My mind is drawn to recent events. Our sister squadron lost an aircraft in the Falklands. The crew made no attempt to eject and their aircraft smashed into Mount Byron with fatal results. Initial reports were sketchy, but within 24 hours the RAF had issued a signal giving only the briefest details – the aircraft serial number, the crew, the position of impact and mission details. It all seems so black and white. Fellow flyers here today but gone tomorrow. It would appear that they had let down through cloud without being 100 per cent sure of their position. Perhaps the INAS was in error, but certain if they had looked at the radar they would have seen they were over land not sea. Perhaps the radar was not working. We shall never know.

Cross-talk front to back is the buzz phrase. As a crew we check the height with regular calls; approaching safety altitude we need to start levelling off. Safety altitude is calculated on the height of the highest object within say 30 miles of calculated position. To that height we add say 1,000 or 2,000 feet as a buffer. We cannot go below that height. For example, over the sea at night with no high ground we use a minimum altitude of 1,000 feet, which is plenty low enough for the faint-hearted! Passing 8,000 feet we can see patches of green fields weaving geometric squares across the North German plain. Aiming for a gap in the clouds my driver deftly puts us into clear air. We are both temporarily disorientated, as nothing seems to fit our mental jigsaw of where we should be. Both of us look desperately for landmarks: a railway line crossing a river, or a town with some distinguishing feature. (All German towns in this area seem to look the same: round in shape with a large church spire poking out from dead centre.) My pilot tells me he can see a lake and about 5 miles beyond is a large 200-foot mast. Happy, I tell him where we are.

'Mike Lima 51, your target has faded last seen 050 degrees range 50.' 'Roger', I reply tersely. My driver pulls the heavy phantom on to 050 degrees. Knowing my driver is happy with our position I can spend more time looking at the radar. He tells me the 'Rad Alt is bugged to 250' – meaning he's set the marker on the radar altimeter to 250 feet. If he descends below that height a red light will illuminate. Backwash calls us. He sounds excited. 'Mike Lima 51, your target is 050 25 miles low level fast.' 'Check switches safe.' My pilot calls back 'Switches safe'. Every action seems to trigger a memory. 'Switches safe' reminds me about an on-going court martial. A crew from our sister squadron have embarrassingly shot down a Jaguar. Scrambled during an exercise with live weapons they engaged their target – a Jaguar fighter-bomber minding his own business RTB to nearby Bruggen. Rolling in behind him the pilot calls good tone Fox 2. Whoosh . . . The crew have forgotten they are live-armed and loosed off a live AIM 9G missile. There is no time to make a radio call before the Sidewinder bandsaws the Jaguar's tail off, as advertised. Fortunately the Jaguar pilot ejected safely. The whole event is embarrassing to say the least. We carefully double-check that we are safe, the trigger is off and the master arm is covered in white tape. As a precaution I have pulled the circuit breaker for the master arm. If we do need to shoot we can be live in less than a second. No sooner has the controller called the contact than the first blip appears on my screen. A small luminous dash slightly fat in the middle. It sits 20 degrees left of our nose. I ask my pilot to move 20 degrees to port. As he rolls the Phantom left the blip centres up and I call him steady. I watch patiently, starting my stopwatch. The blip moves inexorably to the left. I call for a starboard turn 30 degrees right this time. The blip is now hovering around the 40 degrees left of the nose mark. I check our speed and call for 450 knots. As the pilot nudges the power levers forward the Phantom soon reaches its target speed. I now spend less time looking out and more time with my head buried in the cockpit. The trick now is to hold the target at 40 degrees off the nose. As we get closer we need to hold a greater angle of bank to keep the target from sliding off the edge of the radarscope. As this critical moment occurs the backseater calls 'wrap it up'. That's the pilot's cue to increase the bank angle and pull the target to the nose. Hopefully I've given him about 4–5 miles' displacement on the target. This will give us two advantages: enough turning room and a bit of stealth in this rapidly deteriorating visibility. As we go into our

Homeward bound, mission accomplished.

final turn I can feel my G-suit inflate, 3 then 4G comes on till we are screaming round the corner. I flick to pulse mode, aware that the blip was last seen 15 degrees left of the nose. I ease the scanner up away from the ground returns. It must be my lucky day. At just over a mile I can see a bright green blip that isn't rushing down the tube at us. I've now got two choices. Try to keep painting him in search mode with the risk of losing him among the ground clutter or lock him up. If I lock him up and he is hostile his radar-warning receiver is going to light up like a Christmas tree. If he's hostile it could be the last we see of him. I decide to stay in search mode. I guide my pilot's eyes on to the target: 5 degrees left at a mile and half, hold 450 knots. The blip is moving slowly down the scope so at least we have some closure. 'TALLY' shouts my pilot as he gets visual contact with the target. 'ID, ID, ID [Identify]', I call to him – I need to know what it is we're chasing. 'Standby' is his reply. 'Check switches safe' – 'Roger, switches safe.' Now is definitely not the time to screw up.

I crane my head. Looking through the left quarter light I can see the target. It's low, very low, a shimmering heat haze billowing behind its jet pipes. 'It's a Lightning!' I had seen enough of this venerable fighter to recognise it from any angle. A little bemused as to why a Lightning should be floating around at low altitude at this early hour my front-seater begins to close up. The pilot does not see us until we loom into his peripheral vision. The Lightning looks different. It's painted a new light grey colour and bears few unit or national markings. As we close up alongside our prey I make a careful note of the finer details such as its serial number, unit badge, position. We call ground control and tell him it's a friendly target identity 'Lightning'. Startled, he tells us to haul off and return to base. Not wishing to leave our single-seat pilot in any doubt as who's the boss my driver cracks the burners in.

Major servicing of the RAF's Phantom force was predominantly carried out at RAF St Athan. However, fairly in-depth work could be carried out at any home base, as is evident in this photo. XV422 is towed back to the aircraft servicing hangar after ground runs.

Night scramble: the pilot and navigator race the groundcrew to the aircraft.

We quickly shoot past our target as he racks on 90 degrees of bank. A Phantom in full reheat showing off its arsenal of weapons is hugely impressive. My pilot keeps the burners in and eases the nose up, pointing towards the blue, blue sky. Earth-bound misfits we are not as we claw back into the safe environment of medium altitude. The INAS is selected to home base and we settle down on track. Our return leg is fairly rapid. We need to get the aircraft back on state, and more to the point we're off duty in one hour. We are handed from one controller to another until we're back with 'Clutch' radar. These are the guys who look after us. Located somewhere in the heart of Dusseldorf, they are fine controllers. We share a mutual respect that every year is reinforced. The annual Clutch beer call has become a legendary event on the fighter squadron's calendar. Crews from the RAFG bases meet up with German Starfighter pilots, ground controllers and NATO allies. We all arrive in our respective nationality's flying apparel. Several hours later most of us are sporting bright orange suits or the uniform of a German administrative officer. (For some bizarre reason, the more intoxicated fighter crews become the more they want to swap clothes.) High-spirited jinks go on till late in the night and gallons of German beer are drunk; eventually we are all bussed home. Early the next day a polite signal arrives on the squadron from the German controllers: 'Could we please have the following items returned. A senior German officer's leather trench coat, two typewriters and the machine-gun from the Panzer tank guarding the gate.' All this was doubtless regarded as legitimate booty but it is all duly returned. Such gatherings give us all a close bond with our ground-based controllers. One day for sure they'll save our necks.

Below me I can see the meandering Rhine bisecting the sprawling suburbs of Dusseldorf and Koln Bonn – time we were descending. I call Clutch and we are cleared down to 6,000 feet on the regional pressure setting. My pilot closes the throttles and pops the speedbrakes out. The Phantom loses the will to fly and the nose drops well below the horizon. I can make out all the familiar landmarks now so I decide to park the radar and ask wings in the front if he's happy to go VFR (Visual Flight Rules). 'Sure' comes back the reply – he's never one to waste words. I tell Clutch that we are calling base and chop to Wildenrath Approach frequency. I call Dolphin Ops, our squadron, just to let them know we'll be down in five minutes and we have a serviceable jet. Our engineers will want to know as soon as possible if we can put the same jet on state. If we have any technical snags they'll need to drag out the spare, which will take time. In some ways the Battle Flight duty is a blessing in disguise to the engineers. Aircraft that are due for servicing but are running out of hours, or aircraft that have used too much fatigue are tucked away and forgotten in the Battle Flight shed. It's a useful way of extending their lives.

Field in sight we call the tower: 'Tower Mike Lima 51 initials break.' 'Roger runway 27 1009.' We both set our altimeters to 1009 and then cross check. I rattle through the arrival checks, making sure we're not going to do anything silly with a live-armed jet. As we nudge down to 800 feet we are 30 seconds from the runway threshold when all hell breaks loose. As our squadron is abeam the threshold I should have twigged what was going to happen next. For some reason I've gone head in, foraging around the cockpit when SMACK, BANG – my bone dome cracks against the side of the canopy. I'm curled up, head to one side, as the onset of G builds up to 4. I try to lift my head, now weighing about four times normal weight. My witty driver calls '51s on the break to land'. While I'm regaining my composure the pilot's hands are flashing around the ergonomic slum in the front – throttles idle, speedbrakes out, stick back to neutral. Catching me unawares, my driver obviously thought it would be very cool to give the boys an early morning wake-up call by breaking right over the squadron. Normally we break halfway down the field. Right now we're at 1,000 feet at 250 knots and the power is reducing; simultaneously I can feel the speedbrakes come in and hear the gear drop down with a resounding clunk. As the speed drops back further I can hear mutterings from in front: 'Flaps, hook, harness.' 'Tight locked,' I reply. 'Taxi light on hydraulics, pneumatics, all OK.' My pilot checks his fuel, calculates his 'ON Speed' and starts a hard descending turn towards the threshold. I can feel a surge of power as he starts the pull and it should be an interesting manoeuvre. From the ground we must look like some prehistoric bird, everything dangling and trailing a grey smoke plume. By 250 feet my pilot has his act together and we're nicely lined up. I check his AOA and see we are 'on the donut'. We cross the threshold and arrive with a thump. There's no need for a flare – after all, it was designed to perform a controlled crash on to a carrier deck. Ahead of us is 8,500 feet of tarmac, then trees. Instinctively I look into the rear view mirror. 'Good Chute', I call, as the dirty white parachute billows out behind us, dragging us to a halt.

As soon as we turn off the runway we both crack open our canopies. The cool fresh morning air is a welcome relief from our claustrophobic confines. We've got nearly a mile and a half to taxi back to our squadron, time to complete the after-landing checks and reflect on the mission. All we've actually done is what we've been trained to do: get our Phantom airborne in under five minutes, intercept a target from low level to 50,000 feet, then report, identify, shadow or DESTROY. Today we just had to identify the target – who knows when or if the call to ENGAGE will come. As we enter the squadron dispersal our fellow fliers are getting ready to launch the day's missions. They seem unfazed by our presence on just another routine scramble. We pull up next to the shelter and turn the mighty Phantom through 90 degrees. Already waiting is the tractor and tow bar ready to push us back into our concrete cavern. In the next hour our groundcrew will refuel, replenish and re-load our Phantom – it has to be back on state within the hour. Shutting down we climb down the ladders to meet the on-coming crew. Making sure nothing is left in the cockpit, my pilot and I part company. He signs the aircraft back in as I make my report to sector control. We are both curious as to why the Lightning had been so far from home.

My controller sounds apologetic. It would appear two Lightnings had been based at Jever in Northern Germany for the past week, taking part in the TLP (Tactical Leadership Programme). The day before one of the Lightnings had landed unserviceable with an engine problem. Working through the night the groundcrew had fixed the problem, and in order to check the engine before the first mission they decided to fly the aircraft as early as possible. Air test complete, the pilot decided to drop down to low altitude before returning to base. Unbeknown to him Herman the Nike missile controller was just getting out of his car when a swept-wing, silverish fighter flew overhead. With no visible markings it looked like an East German SU22 Fitter. Fearing that one had strayed across the border he rang sector control and Battle Flight was duly launched. It was an understandable mistake as the two aircraft do look remarkably similar. I am slightly concerned that in the event of war this man will have to differentiate between a Jaguar and a Soviet Flogger – again, one is a dead ringer for the other.

Almost ten years to the day from this scramble on 2 October 1991 the last ever Battle Flight scramble by a Phantom in Germany took place. With the Cold War finally over, the RAF closed another chapter in its famous history.

CHAPTER 6

Memories of the F4

Cliff Spink

I joined the F4 world at the time the aircraft was moving from the strike ground attack role to air defence, having previously spent my operational career on the Lightning. I well remember walking out for my first ever trip with a navigator. Luckily Willy Felger was already very experienced in the low-level role with both the RAF and the German Air Force. 'Well, Spinko,' he said, 'I know b— all about Air Defence and you know b— all about the F4, but together we might just about survive this sortie!' We did, and it was to be the start of an association with an aircraft that gave me some of the most stimulating flying imaginable.

Plan view of a 56 Squadron FGR2 flying low over a pea-green North Sea. This was the definitive grey scheme for RAF Phantoms: light grey with darker grey upper wing surfaces. Standard for UK crews was the white Mk 4 bone dome.

This close formation barrel role proves that the Phantom was more nimble than its looks suggested.

Formation flying has always been synonymous with fighter squadrons, ever since the days of the Hendon air pageants. Flying in close proximity to other aircraft has always been a skill required by air defence pilots.

Air combat also goes hand-in-hand with fighter squadrons. For the pilots, nothing was better than spending two weeks in sun-soaked climes taking on other NATO jets. Here a row of clean Phantoms rest after a hard day's combat.

Without its tanks the Phantom looked as good as any other classic jet.

In truth my initial impressions of the aircraft were not entirely positive; the take-off was impressive enough with the reheated Speys chucking out more than enough thrust to allow the aircraft to defy gravity, but out of 'burner' I found her a bit ponderous and the cold power climb was a joke. However, in her proper environment – fast and with the power up – the aircraft could give you the ride of a lifetime. At last we had an interceptor with a lot of fuel and weapons, plus a radar that gave us all-aspect performance, particularly at low level. I had always enjoyed air combat training and knew, from fighting against the F4 in the Lightning, that in competent hands the Phantom was a formidable opponent. That said, the skills required in the cockpit were different, not least at a high angle of attack (AOA). With ailerons that only went down (although purists insist they did go up a degree or so!), and a spoiler on the down-going wing, at high AOA a roll towards an opponent using just the stick would result in entirely the opposite effect – and very dramatic it was too! So the technique was to keep the stick still and roll the aircraft using the rudder – 'fighting with your feet'. Early combat sorties could be frustrating as it was easy to revert to techniques hard-won on other aircraft. In a high-G turning fight, as your opponent lowered his nose to gain some energy, it was easy to forget and match his move by rolling into the turn using the stick . . . in a heartbeat your steed flicks the

Not all sorties ran on rails. This pair of OCU jets are inches from disaster. With the leader on the left the student on the right attempts to swap sides at a critical moment. Caught in the full power slipstream of the leader's Speys he loses control. More by luck than skill he ends up on the other side pointing in the right direction.

Without the groundcrew the F4s would have remained firmly on the ground. They were designed in an era when reliability was not a key issue and the engineers worked long hours to keep the mighty Phantom in the skies.

A Germany Phantom on final approach to Akrotiri after a 5-hour transit. Centreline tanks were the normal fit for the UK squadrons except for long-range transits.

other way and a few seconds later you would be soaking up a Fox 2 from your opponent. This was not good for crew morale and would result in pilots buying a lot of beer for their grumpy navigators, who didn't like losing! Nor did I, and I soon learnt how to get the optimum from this aircraft – if only to protect my monthly bar bill! Fly fast, but know your best turning speed; use the vertical; practise good crew cooperation; optimise the weapon system; and know when to engage and disengage – these became my credo with the Phantom – although 'Sailor' Malan's *Ten Rules for Air Fighting* also still applied. Combat became a joy, but there was much more to the F4, and it was its breadth of capacity and flexibility that made it such a demanding but rewarding aircraft to fly.

Sorties from Leuchars to intercept Soviet bombers encroaching into the UK Air Defence Region became a regular feature of operations for the two squadrons – 111(F) and 43(F) – and it was unusual for crews on QRA not to scramble north to shadow the mighty Bear aircraft. Frustratingly for me, the Soviets stayed at home when I was on duty, and as the months of my tour progressed the junior crews on my flight easily beat me to the award of the '10 Bear badge' – a red star on which was superimposed the Russian bear with the figure '10' on its chest. I eventually broke my duck and it was worth waiting for – you could actually hear the drone of those massive contra-rotating props from within the F4 cockpit, and the sheer size of the aircraft, by the standards of the day, was very impressive. I duly got my badge – a red star on which was superimposed a *teddy*-bear with the figure '2' on its chest! I did eventually get my '10', including one memorable night sortie under the Northern

Colour returned to the Phantom force in the later years. Here 56 and 74 Squadrons are showing how fighter aircraft should look!

Firebird showmanship at its best!

In the 1970s and 1980s the F4 was a common sight in Europe. Many sorties were flown against other Phantoms, and in an effort to differentiate between the good guys and the bad guys some RAF F4s were painted with temporary high visibility markings.

This unique formation marked the retirement of Sir Patrick Hine. A Lightning, two Hunters, a Harrier and two F4s joined together as a tribute to the types he had flown in RAF service.

Lights. The luminous and shifting green sky was breathtaking, but in a heavy Phantom in the QRA fit of three tanks and eight missiles, plugged in behind a Victor tanker, it could be a mite disorientating! Often, when you had finished shadowing the bad guys, you would be hundreds of miles from the UK and a long time from a hot breakfast – but the F4 engendered a great deal of trust and I always felt that it would get me home. Mind you, finishing a final air-to-air refuelling somewhere closer to Greenland than Britain, and then watching the Victor K2 climb to 40,000 feet and speed home, while we staggered up to 28,000 feet to start a fairly slow and bum-aching transit, did make me wonder again about our lack of cold-power performance at height. However, I was later to fly an F4 in RAF service that did not suffer such a drop in high-level performance – the 'J'.

To command your own squadron is always an honour, but for me it was unique as the squadron was 74(F), *The Tigers*, equipped with the F4J. Obtained to fill the gap left by the deployment of another squadron to the Falklands, these ex-US Navy aircraft were brought out of their desert storage, refurbished to 'S' standard and quickly

Many F4 pilots had previously flown the Lightning in service. They brought with them a huge knowledge of intercept theory and of course fuel awareness!

Up to 25 per cent of Phantom missions were flown at night, with the UK squadrons performing significantly more than the Germany squadrons.

The Phantom could have soldiered on for a few more years before it was retired. With the reduced threat of war it was decided not to pursue further upgrades and the type was fully replaced by the Tornado F3 by 1992.

At one stage both the Wildenrath wings' two-stickers were non-RWR dirty grey machines. They are seen here together in the Wildenrath revetments built for the Sabres of the 1950s.

BA
XT873

flown to Wattisham, their new home. I took over the squadron from Dick Northcote and was delighted when I first flew this model of the F4. The 'J' certainly took longer to get airborne than the Spey-powered variants; indeed, following an F4M in a pairs take-off resulted in him being airborne with his wheels already tucked away while you were still firmly on the runway. (For getting a heavily laden F4K off the relatively small aircraft carriers of the Royal Navy it had made some sense to have more initial oomph.) That for me was the only performance advantage of the F4K/M and once airborne I felt the J79-powered 'J' was much superior in the air defence role. The pure jet power, instant reheat, smaller intakes and original area ruling of the airframe made for an altogether more sprightly machine and at last we had some high-level performance without having to be stuck in reheat. In addition, we flew with just the centre external tank, which gave us all the endurance we required for a normal sortie without the penalty of a reduced G limit. It was a rare treat to do a two against two combat sortie against the Binbrook Lightnings and, to their surprise, bounce them from above – when they were at their normal start point of 36,000+ feet.

It was during this time that someone on the squadron suggested an attempt on the London–Edinburgh speed record, which at that time was held by a Jaguar. The Jaguar had flown overland at the highest subsonic speed allowed, without dropping a sonic boom. Our options were to do the same and rely on better tailwinds to break the record, or to go the longer distance up the east coast which would allow us to use the full supersonic performance of the aircraft. We chose the latter course and on 1 July 1987 two F4Js made the attempt. I flew ZE351 'India' with navigator Sqn Ldr Steve Smyth, and Flt Lts Ian 'Stilts' Gale and Ned Kelly were in the second aircraft. With the FAI monitoring our

First to be retired were the tired Leuchars-based FG1s. For some reason the 92 Squadron blue-tailed FGR2 has slipped in among this mass graveyard of FG1s.

Crews were often authorised for Targets of Opportunity (TOO). This simply meant they got airborne, went to CAP and had a go at anything which transited their airspace – carefree days indeed!

attempt we crossed the London line in our clean F4Js shortly after topping off with fuel from a Victor. The transit over East Anglia was a fast, but legal, subsonic cruise but as we crossed the Norfolk coast we accelerated to about Mach 1.6. From then on it was a case of watching the rapidly dropping fuel gauges, and balancing our speed against our ability to get safely back to Leuchars once we had crossed the Edinburgh line. We beat the existing record by less than a minute, crossing the line in a time of 27 minutes 3 seconds. As we taxied on to the chocks at Leuchars I looked in amazement at the other 'J' – the paint had been stripped from the back of the aircraft. I know our aircraft looked the same because Stilts and Ned were staring in our direction with the same open mouths. Ah well, Group HQ had told me that I had too many 74 Squadron aircraft with black tails!

The Phantom was a truly great aircraft, and the RAF crews that flew this most capable fighter knew that if the Cold War ever got hotter then this was the cockpit to be in.

CHAPTER 7

Nick's Scottish Phantom

Nick Anderson

The squadron had deployed up to Kinloss for several months while the runway at Leuchars was resurfaced. It was great being right in the middle of one of the best low-flying regions in the country so we took every opportunity we could to get down into the weeds. Even when we had to work over the North Sea flying intercepts we would get there at low level, but only if we didn't waste too much gas doing it.

Budgie and I were on our way to fly intercepts against an old Shackleton and we were easing our way over the rolling hills at a couple of hundred feet. I was keeping the speed back to lower the fuel consumption, not a clever trick considering I had a couple of wing tanks and a centreline

Phantom silhouette. Framed against a low winter sun a tooled-up F4 returns to base.

Most Phantom crews were posted to the F3 or to other duties at the end of the Phantom era. Few crews held the Tornado in such high regard as the legendary F4.

Low level in the mountains – on a clear day nothing could be more fun. In winter in Scotland it could be a very demanding environment for both pilot and navigator.

tank weighing the aircraft down. I drifted into a gently winding valley enjoying the feeling of weaving the Phantom back and forth. The turns became a little harder as the valley tightened up and I already had full military power to keep my airspeed up but without realising it my speed was slowly dropping. After a couple of tight turns with my canopy brushing the rocks I found that the end of the valley was suddenly upon me, a sheer wall of rock stretching up into the sky. I eased back on the stick but the aircraft was reacting slowly and the angle of attack was building quickly. For a split second I thought of tapping the burners but with our temperamental Spey engines the afterburner light-up took several seconds and in the meantime the nozzles would open slightly, reducing thrust. I kept the pressure on the stick until the pedal shaker started rattling under my foot. The nose was still coming up but I didn't know if we were going to clear the ridge or not. I was holding my breath. A gap between some pines gave me a way through into clear sky. I clenched the cheeks of my ass waiting for the back of the aircraft to clip the rock but we crept through smoothly, kicking up a cloud of dust as the exhausts seared the ground.

I lit up the burners to get flying speed back and hauled the Phantom safely up to 10,000 feet. Budgie asked what the problem was; he had been head down watching the tube and hadn't realised just how close I had come to smearing us over a lump of granite. I sat there in a cold sweat wondering if it might not be a good idea if I gave it all up . . . but soon the confidence of youth began to reassert itself. As lessons go, however, it was a hard one.

We had FG1 Phantoms on 43(F) Squadron, some RAF and the rest ex-Navy ones from the old *Ark Royal*. They were a bit of a nightmare, with some rather important bits and pieces missing. The FG1 didn't have a parking brake, battery or HF radio; nor, in the early days, did it have a gyro gunsight. Nor did we have an INAS, just a clockwork box of tricks that usually had us in the wrong hemisphere, let alone in the UK! More than one navigator was led astray but one crew in particular was caught out on a QRA mission. Well out of position and low on fuel, they dumped eight missiles and three fuel tanks into the Atlantic and headed for home. They wouldn't have made it but for the fortuitous arrival of a tanker which gave them enough gas to limp back to Leuchars.

The F4 was a big, big fighter, mean-looking and aggressive. The cockpit was meaty, with little subtlety and plenty of sharp corners. The controls were large and imposing with everything shaped and crafted to aid recognition and function. The only one I really didn't like was the drag chute handle. It needed a strong pull to lift it up but if the pilot were to struggle and let it drop slightly before getting it latched into position the chute was deployed and then unceremoniously dumped on to the runway! The main Attitude Indicator was a work of art. It showed bank and pitch but would also rotate to give heading as well. How it

The author's favourite Phantom photo. XV430 is bathed in a wonderful luminescence as she skips across a scudding winter cloud top.

Vertical plan form. I'd always wanted to create this image but never had the chance. At the end of 56 Squadron I was given a Hawk ably flown by ex-F4 driver Jos Fenton. With seasoned Phantom pilot Mike Parkin in the clean-wing FGR2 I decided to give it a go. It's actually a very hard image to capture. You need a good horizon to give the correct impression. You need to pick the pull-up heading carefully to ensure that as the aircraft performs a vertical spot roll it is correctly highlighted. This almost relaxed-looking pose hides the fact that shortly afterwards both Phantom and Hawk fell out of the sky, out of energy and ideas!

was geared I have no idea but it was beautiful and I always enjoyed instrument flying in the Phantom.

When we bought the F4 from the Americans the British government insisted on using Rolls-Royce engines and they chose the Spey. As an airliner engine, it wasn't really suited to the job and although it was supposed to be more powerful than the original it was heavier and wider. What we ended up with was the slowest, heaviest and most expensive F4 in the world. The radar we used was good and in its time it was probably the best AI radar in the world. It was hard for the backseaters, particularly when running in search mode against low-level targets, as the display showed azimuth and speed but no range! One great disadvantage was the lack of an internal gun. If we wanted to go to war with our

As a backseater it was a fantastic experience to have such a superb view. Paul 'Gandhi' Willis holds rock steady formation seconds away from a pairs landing.

20mm cannon (firing 100 rounds a second) we had to mount it on the centreline station and leave the fuel tank at home.

Flying the Phantom was always a challenge and there wasn't an F4 pilot alive who didn't respect it. While it was a handful, it was conventional to fly until you tried to manoeuvre at high AOA (angle of attack). In this case, if the stick was used to roll the aircraft the ailerons would cause so much adverse yaw that the aircraft could roll the wrong way and might even depart into a spin – not a good idea in the F4. So as the AOA came up to around 19 units the technique was to keep the ailerons central and roll the aircraft using the rudder – not an easy skill to master, especially in a fight.

The F4 was the first aircraft I flew that had a tail hook. Big and reliable, it rarely skipped the cable and was often used to prevent overruns after brake failures or aquaplaning. The first time I remember using it in anger was on a dirty wet night when the wind had risen above crosswind limits. With 35 knots across the runway my venerable and experienced backseater Tony suggested that tonight was a good time to see how it felt flying into the approach end cable. With the hook dangling well below the aircraft I didn't want to plough up any approach lights so I crabbed in right on the red/whites of the VASIs. The wire plucked the F4 from the air before the main wheels were properly on to the ground and as we thumped into the runway I bit my tongue. The wire jerked the aircraft straight and with my nose up against the gunsight we came safely to a halt. I've had worse landings but rarely bled as much for them!

The wings could be folded to save space (or to wave at Air Traffic as we taxied past) but, as one guy found out in Germany, it wouldn't fly very well with them unlocked. RAF Germany seemed to have its fair share of incidents with the F4. Probably the most famous was the day a very unfortunate crew flying on an exercise with live missiles shot down a Jaguar. The Jag pilot survived and ejected to safety but the F4 crew had a lot of explaining to do. The Phantom involved in this impromptu test firing now resides as the gate guard at RAF Stornoway and the whole story can be found written on the inside of the radome.

CHAPTER 8

Low-Level Air Defence

Ian Black

The Phantom's origins as an air defence fighter began some six years before its change of role. In June 1970 Phantoms began replacing the Canberra bombers with 14, 17 and 31 Squadrons. Standing alone, 2 (Army Co-operation) Squadron gave up its single-seat Hunter FR10s at Gutersloh and went twin-seat with the FGR2 from December 1970. Interestingly, despite the designation FGR2, only around thirty aircraft were actually capable of carrying the external recce pod. It was always planned that the RAF Germany aircraft would be a stopgap. The Anglo-French Jaguar fighter-bomber was planned to replace the Phantom from the outset. Although the Jaguar was much smaller than the Phantom it was none the less well suited to the role. When the Phantom entered service in Germany its primary role was in support of allied ground forces on the North German plain. With its excellent range, targets far over the border were well within its reach. Additionally the multi-role Phantoms were capable of nuclear strike missions. Like the Buccaneers and Tornados that followed, they were designed to work without tanker support. Missions were always planned without the use of air-to-air refuelling.

The first Phantom unit proper to form in RAFG was 14 Squadron. Allocated to SACEUR (Supreme Allied Commander Europe) within the envelope of 2ATAF (2nd Allied Tactical Air Force), it formed at Bruggen on 1 July 1970. Next to form was 17(F) Squadron, which officially formed on 1 September 1970. Last of the Bruggen units was 31 Squadron, another Canberra operator, which took longer to become operational owing to a shortage of crews and aircraft. Indeed this period was to be the lowest point in the history of RAF Phantom operations. Severe engine problems resulted in a slowdown in the output of 228 OCU. Whole courses were cancelled elsewhere. The front-line squadrons took priority on spare engines with the OCU suffering badly in consequence. In fact so acute was the problem that the RAF re-formed two Hunter squadrons, 45 and 58, just to keep pilots current as well as honing new fighter pilots' skills. Some navigators during the same period were posted to other types and never saw service on the Phantom for the rest of their careers. Finally, 31 Squadron declared themselves operational on 7 October 1971. Although 31 Squadron's secondary role was photo-reconnaissance, one unit was dedicated entirely to this role. With RAF Bruggen firmly established as RAFG's main Phantom base, only one further Phantom unit was operational. No. 2 AC (Army

Normally we flew in pairs a mile or two apart depending on the weather. Germany crews often had to fly in appalling visibility making it very hard to keep formation. That said, the Germany F4 crews were some of the best air defenders in the world. Had the Warsaw Pact attacked, the F4s would have certainly scored numerous kills.

Once a year each squadron would take four or five aircraft and perform a squadron exchange with one of our NATO allies. Up in the Arctic Circle Julian Stinton and Andy Kirk drop into a blue ice glacier.

To save fuel, transits to the play area were often flown at medium level. Down at 250 feet fuel consumption can be twice that at 30,000 feet.

John Connor, a former Phantom aerobatic pilot, with Pete Gilmour in the back lifts off from Wildenrath's rain-soaked tarmac in the winter of 1983.

Co-operation) Squadron at RAF Laarbruch was dedicated to the photorecce role. The sole Phantom simulator was based at RAF Bruggen so all operators passed through this point. Initially delivered in typical 1960s glossy camouflage, the Phantoms were quick to tone down. The paint schemes became matt and wherever possible white was removed. The Phantoms were to be the spearhead in a new, tense Cold War period.

The Phantom's attack role in Germany was extremely short-lived. By April 1975 Jaguars had begun arriving at Bruggen and 14 Squadron ceased flying Phantoms by the end of that year. Quick to follow were 17 and 31 Squadrons and by the summer of 1976 all the Phantoms had been replaced.

The Phantom was, however, set to serve in Germany for a further sixteen years. Giving up its Lightning F2As, 19 Squadron re-equipped with the FGR2 in January 1977. Using machines formerly operated by the now defunct 2 Squadron they were quickly joined by 92 (East India) Squadron. RAF Wildenrath became the new home of RAFG's air defence force. RAF Germany's commitment to NATO during this period was the policing of the ADIZ (Air Defence Interception Zone), with the Phantoms being responsible for the northern sector. This was, however, a peacetime role. In war the Phantom's main task was to plug any gaps in the Hawk/Nike missile belt. This belt of low-altitude missiles lay ahead of the RAF's own Rapier missiles used for airfield defence. Initially the FGR2s were more than a match for anything in the NATO inventory. With its two-man crew, superior radar and impressive weapons suite the Wildenrath wing was a force to be reckoned with. In the late 1970s the F104 Starfighter formed the backbone of NATO's front line but it was easily outclassed by the superior British Phantom, which even outdid the American and German Phantoms operating in Europe. All this of course changed when the F15 Eagle and F16 Falcon began to arrive in large numbers. These more agile fighters could outperform the FGR2, although it still had several advantages: its two-man crew, superb low-level radar and radar-guided missiles.

In the mid-1980s the RAF's Phantom force adopted an overall grey scheme. The process was slow, aircraft only being repainted when they needed to be.

Fire crews learning how to remove an injured navigator from the back seat of his Phantom. They also needed to be trained in how to make the ejector seat safe.

Flying low as the pilot tries to get a visual pick-up on his target.

A classic head-on view of the British Phantom.

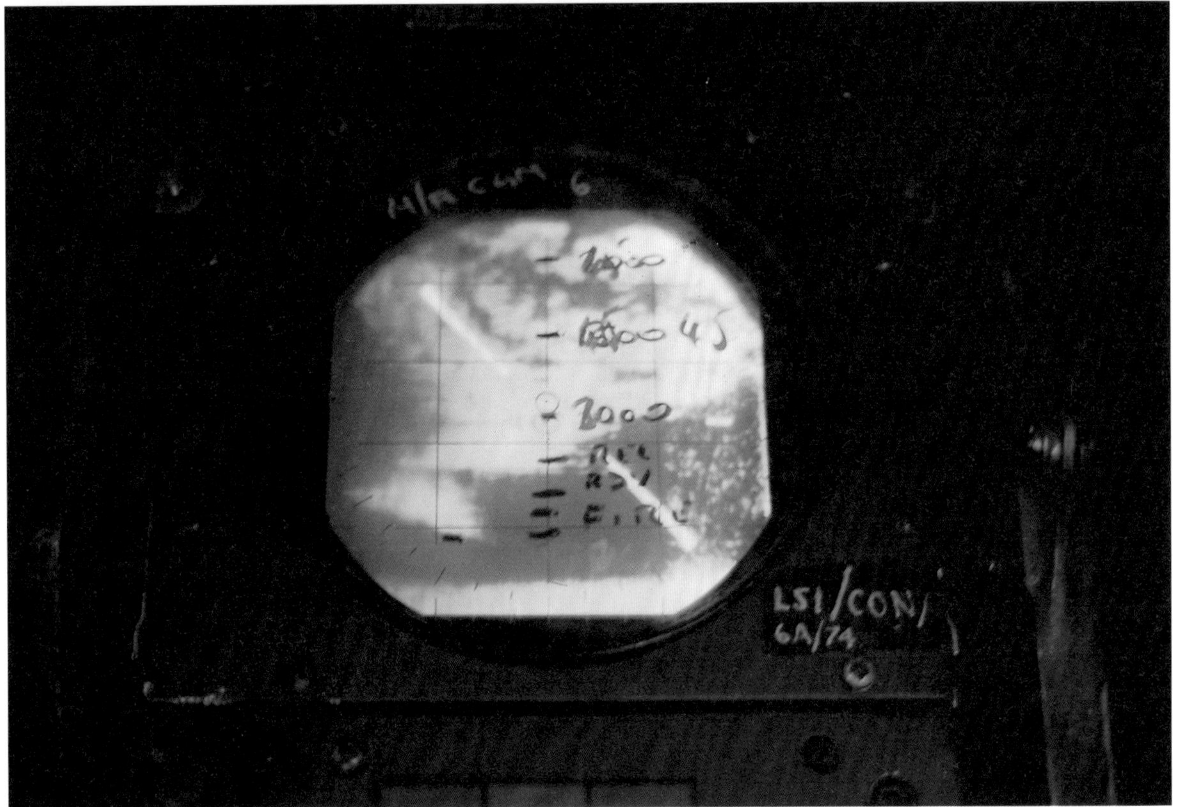

Taking a picture of the radar was quite difficult, not least because in the early 1980s a lot of the information was classified. This is a pulse display showing Cyprus. The sea is black and the coast fluorescent green. Horizon bars are overlaid on the screen to give the backseater an idea of attitude. This particular display also has yellow chinagraph markings overlaid for air-to-air gunnery. As the target 'travelled' down the scope the navigator would call out the actions.

A clean-wing Cold War warrior at low altitude. In this fit the Phantom looked aggressive and purposeful.

Squadron Life

A posting to RAF Germany was always considered a plum job – tax-free living, German beer and some of the best flying around! Before arriving in Germany crews naturally had to get past the staff of 228 OCU based at Coningsby and in latter years at RAF Leuchars. The course ran for nearly six months and gave crews a basic grasp of flying the Phantom. Operating the F4 was down to the individual squadrons. The UK squadrons had the vast North Sea as their playground while RAFG had the North German plain. The OCU course consisted of initial pilot conversion, basic intercepts, air combat and finally advanced intercepts, but none of this prepared the ab initio pilot or navigator for the harsh realities of squadron life. On arrival in Germany the first thing which struck you was how serious the game had become. Bases were guarded by armed troops in combat clothing and tin hats. Everything was painted green in an effort to make the airfield as inconspicuous as possible. Arriving at the squadron it was hard to tell where the buildings were as everything blended into the scenery. Aircraft were housed in first generation HAS (Hardened Aircraft Shelters). Operations buildings were hardened concrete shelters impervious to bomb and gas attack. Our offices, crew rooms and engineering headquarters were all 'soft'.

Initial flying was all deemed to be 'Convex' – conversion exercises. After the obligatory briefings on airspace, rules, standard operating procedures and so on it was normally off to the simulator. It was located at RAF Bruggen, a good half-hour's drive away by squadron mini. Part of the fun of going to the simulator was in trying to break the squadron record of 23 minutes door to door. The awkward part was trying to decide

Low-level beat-up. John Cliffe leads Paul Willis over a small grass airfield on the Venice lido during the summer of 1983.

who was going to drive! Pilots always wanted to occupy the front seat! The simulator itself was a throwback from the days when Bruggen was a Phantom base. It was painted black and looked very sinister, perhaps reflecting its past as a nuclear trainer. Staffed by seasoned ex-Phantom crews, it could replicate the FGR2 in every respect although it lacked any visual displays. In essence it was always flown as if in cloud, on instruments. Prior to each new phase of the conversion pilots and navigators would fly the same profile in the simulator before the airborne exercise. Then it was time to fly. For a backseater the first Phantom flight in Germany was always called a 'Famex' or familiarisation exercise. You sat down with a seasoned pilot and gazed at this strange map as he talked you through all the low-level combat air patrol areas, diversion airfields and (importantly) what to avoid. As a backseater it was important to note the latitude and longitude of all the various waypoints that you'd fly over. These could then be inserted into the Inertial Navigation computer to give you range and bearing information on your selected destination. Briefing would take place inside the hardened accommodation and this was followed by an out-briefing given by the duty authorisation officer. He would ask what we were planning to do, where we were heading and what our alternative plan was should something change. He also gave us our aircraft details, such as where it was located and what configuration it was in.

A 92 Squadron Phantom recovers to Wildenrath after a low-level intercept mission.

Low-level intercepts normally involved a flat fight so it was rare to see people pitching into the vertical. Here a 92 Squadron F4 tries desperately to get a guns kill on us as we pull up into the vertical.

As well as pylons, other aircraft, balloons, kites and the weather, birds are a constant threat at low level. This is the result of hitting a small bird at 450 miles an hour at 250 feet. This required a simple repair, but had it hit the fuselage the aircraft would have been grounded for weeks.

No. 19 Squadron's flagship gets airborne with a Britannia Airways 737 in the background. For many years Britannia Airways had the contract for ferrying troops between the UK and RAF Germany. To the right of the 737 are the Hunting Percival Pembrokes, also a familiar sight at Wildenrath.

This was normally pretty standard as we always flew in the same fit: two external fuel tanks, centreline gun, forward dummy Sparrows and a single drill Sidewinder missile. Having collected our flying clothing from the Portakabin we then passed through the engineers' building where the pilot signed for our allocated Phantom. Each aircraft was only a short walk from the engineers' building, either located in one of the hardened shelters or occasionally parked in one of the three revetments left over from the 1950s. At the OCU there are rows and rows of Phantoms on an enormous concrete apron. Here, the first thing you realise is how cramped the Phantom is inside its shelter. Inside each individual hangar is all the equipment needed to operate the Phantom for several days during war. Spare fuel tanks are stacked against the wall, together with a complete gun. Sidewinder missiles sit waiting to be loaded. An enormous ground power unit is already plugged into the underbelly of the Phantom, giving it electrical energy. The noise level is much higher than I've experienced before and it's hard even to think inside the shelter. My pilot chats to the groundcrew while I shin up the ladder to check the switches in the back cockpit. Before I do anything I need to make sure the rear ejector seat is safe – the thought of being catapulted into the HAS room is not pleasant. I make sure the radar is off and all the circuit breakers are made. As soon as I'm done I do my tightrope act and clamber gingerly into the front, holding tight to the front cockpit rail for fear of falling. My job as navigator is really a safety check of the front cockpit before power is applied. I check the fuel panel, throttles and landing gear and ensure all the weapons switches are safe. Finally I confirm that both generators are off. Clambering back into the rear seat I begin what will become a familiar ritual over the next three years. At first the whole procedure seems unhumanly complicated, aligning the Inertial, strapping in and talking on the radio. Three years on and I'll wonder what all the fuss is about. Adding to my

Cruising round the hilly Low Flying Area 3, this fully armed Phantom is on a practice scramble. After the accidental shooting down of a Jaguar, crews were very wary of flying live-armed aircraft.

Our probe nicely frames XV439, plugged into the starboard Victor hose.

In the mid-1980s crews were offered tanker support for everyday missions – an added bonus for Germany crews. Unlike the UK squadrons, all the tanking there was performed at altitude overland. The beautiful shape of 44 Squadron Vulcan XL445 is apparent in this image.

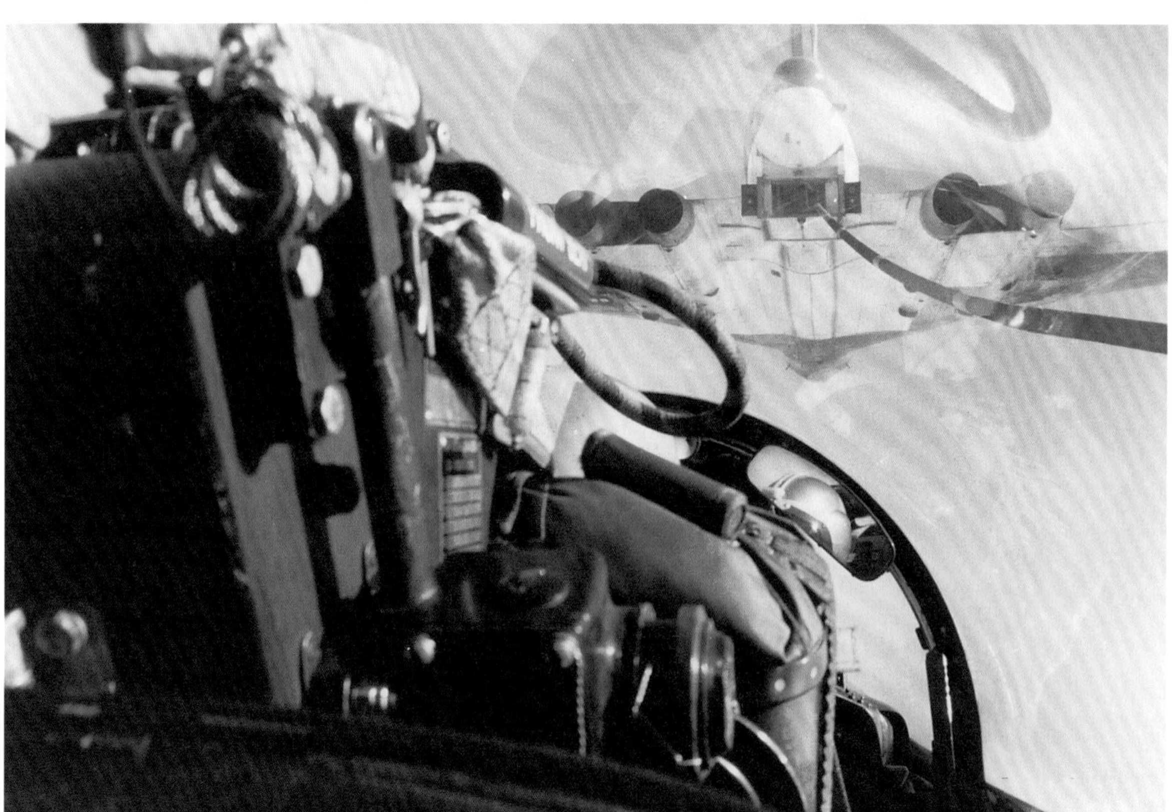

The view from the back, taking on fuel from the hastily converted Vulcan bombers.

complete lack of agility is the fact that it's nearly a month since I last flew. After a fashion I get all my waypoints into the Inertial; my pilot is already prepared, engines running, waiting for Mr Slowcoach in the back to get his act together. I can almost hear him tapping his fingers on the canopy arch, willing me to hurry up. Confirming all is ready we call for taxi and my pilot inches the throttles forward. The Phantom roars. The two Spey engines are barely more than idling but the noise inside the HAS is deafening. I glance nervously at each wing tip as we trundle into the clear. My pilot starts to turn left, nosewheel steering engaged. Either side of us are the revetment walls. A yellow line is painted on the concrete to guide us safely to the taxiway. It seems pretty easy to me. (Much later I flew with Mick, a fellow first tourist in the twin sticker. Knowing I want to be a driver he lets me taxi the mighty Phantom back from a sortie. All goes well till we enter the revetment – whereupon he seizes control just seconds before I mangle the Phantom's outer wing panel on the concrete. Maybe it's not so easy!) As we enter the taxiway I'm far too busy to take in my surroundings, and all I can see is trees. We run through the pre-take-off checks and cross to tower frequency. With canopies cracked open the cold March air stings the small piece of flesh between mask and helmet. As we near the runway we can see the north side of the airfield. Parked to one side are the Hunting Percival Pembrokes, twin piston-engined communications aircraft. They look rather out of place, painted in Transport Command's blue, white and grey. Still they look the part. Who would know even in peacetime that they play a vital role flying up and down the Berlin corridor . . . but who knows what they *really* do. Coiled barbed wire segregates the dispersal from the airfield as we line up on the westerly runway. I call out the runway checklist:

'Pitot Heat' – 'On.'

'Wings' – 'Spread and locked.' (I check visually.)

'Flaps' – 'Half.'

'Stab Aug Switches' – 'ENGAGED.'

Lending aircraft to your sister squadron was always a risky business! XV411 has had the full Cobra treatment applied to its starboard drop-tank.

Photographed from another Phantom, XV472 launches a live Skyflash missile against a radar target off the Welsh coast.

Outside the hardened shelter groundcrew run through the pre-flight servicing schedule.

Zapped by 100 Squadron, John Goddard strikes a pose in the front cockpit of well-worn XV480.

'Anti Skid Switch' – 'On Caption out.'
'Engine Checks' – 'All within Limits.'
'Warning Lights' – 'All Out.'
'Ramps' – 'Retracted.'

Once we are cleared for take-off the pilot releases the brakes, engages the burner and the mighty Phantom rolls forward. The acceleration isn't massive; well, it is 1981 and the Phantom first flew twenty-three years ago. What *is* impressive is the constant thrust. As the speed builds we flash past Air Traffic and rotate. As the nose rises and we break ground I can see the main entrance to the station in my peripheral vision. I'm reminded of my first glimpse of the station, with a sign reading 'Welcome to Royal Air Force Wildenrath. The purpose of this station in peace is to train for war.' As we accelerate into the ether I'm in no doubt as to why I'm doing this. Yes it's fun but it's also a vocation. Like the rest of the squadron, we're all in this together, training in peace to fly the Phantom in war. Our mission today seems far removed from the harsh realities of modern warfare. We might just as well be in a Cessna bumbling along on an afternoon navex. The fact is every time we strap into the Phantom we are gaining valuable air time. After

Everything down, XV470 flies over the 56 Squadron dispersal.

Transiting back from low level as the sun sets is FGR2 XV437, which was eventually lost in a flying accident.

about eighteen months it will be like putting on an old glove. No longer will it take me an age to align the INAS when I strap myself to the Martin Baker seat; it will be more like putting a car seatbelt on. Using the radar will be like tuning the radio. Every action will become second nature. Importantly I won't need to think about my actions. All my spare brain capacity can be put to good use, dividing my attention between radar and look-out position. At the same level my pilot will handle the Phantom without thought, flying by instinct. He won't put us into unrecoverable situations because mastering the F4 is what it's all about.

As we leave the Wildenrath zone I have a horrid feeling of missing the bus. After so long off flying at such a young age it's all a bit bewildering. The trick, gained only with experience, is to concentrate on what's important at the time. At this stage I leave the radar alone and concentrate on navigating. My pilot is a seasoned aviator; John has nearly a thousand hours on the Phantom and could fly this route with his eyes closed. Despite the ten-year age gap he's very understanding, pointing out various landmarks that will be useful for the next three years. The RAF hospital at Wegberg flashes under the right wing, a big circular building in grey concrete surrounded by woods with a lake. Mentally I store it away. One day in the future to be sure I'll need that photographic image. Because we are so steely we fly in all weathers; in fact we fly beyond the limit. The RAF low-flying rules state that we need 5 km forward visibility and 1,000 feet clear of cloud. Anyone who's ever flown in the Rhineland will quickly appreciate that if we stuck to these rules we'd be grounded 90 per cent of the time! Today the weather is good as we continue to head north. Next on our list is the imposing building known as Headquarters RAF Germany. Dipping down to 250 feet and holding 420 knots John flies us right over the main door of this bureaucratic monolith. A smile creeps across my face as 25 tons of screaming Phantom flashes across this administrative haven. My mind conjures an image of an administration officer spilling his Earl Grey tea. We push north. As we cross the Rhine John tells me to put the map away and get the radar out. For a backseater this is a three-handed job. On my left side is the black control panel, which pulls out from its recess. On it are about twenty knobs, dials and switches. It looks more like a Belling cooker than a piece of military hardware. Each switch is different, some knurled, some smooth, some rotary. With time I'll be able to operate all the switches and dials without putting my head in the cockpit. I need to keep looking out. Spotting other targets is half the game; if we are spotted first then we need to take action. I have to assess the target to see what level of evasive jink we need to perform. If the target is far away I may just ask my frontseater to manoeuvre the aircraft into a better position to make an intercept. If the target is close I may just call 'BREAK!' left or right. As my pilot kicks in the burners and throws us into a max rate turn I'll be starting my running commentary from the back seat, describing the type of aircraft, range, whether he's a threat, whether he's about to take a gun or missile shot and so on. I need to convey to my driver as succinctly as possible just how close we are to becoming a painted silhouette on the enemy's fuselage. This really is where flying in RAFG moves into widescreen. The picture here is very real and everyone is playing the same deadly serious game. Statistics prove it. A Phantom flies into a mountain trying to avoid being shot down in mock combat; a Harrier flies into the ground turning hard while trying to evade a Phantom. This is the price we pay to be the best. As we cruise north-eastwards we see lots of other fighters and fighter-bombers: the sky is littered with NATO hardware. John points out the main features as we cross the Osnabruck ridge – setting for many a future air battle. As we transit through the low-flying areas our height and speed are constant: 250 feet above ground level at 420 knots. At this height we work as a team, John looking out, me navigating and operating the radar. We swing south and head for Area 3, the Eiffel Mountains. These are more like big hills to anyone from Scotland but they are still a stark contrast to the flat German plain. Here we need to fly higher to stand any chance of seeing targets on radar as they scurry through the gorges and valleys. Our fuel is now running low and we need to head for base. If I were a new pilot I'd be flying the same route but with an experienced navigator in the back. The transit back to base is uneventful and John puts us back where we started from some ninety minutes previous. The start of three years' Phantom flying has begun.

Armament Practice Camp

Perhaps the highlight for any air defence squadron is the annual detachment to RAF Akrotiri in Cyprus. Each squadron will deploy there for one calendar month and hone their skills at air-to-air gunnery. Before we go the squadron engineers will be hard at work as usual, making sure that ten of our Phantoms are prepared for a month-long stint away from base. Servicings are carried out early, guns are harmonised, and centreline fuel tanks are fitted. While the engineers are busy preparing the Phantoms the aircrew are busy being lectured to death on Phantom weapons. It's only six weeks since I joined the squadron and already my Phantom hours have doubled to eighty. Since leaving the OCU I've seen the mighty F4 in a new light, engaging in low-level overland intercepts, air-to-air refuelling, air tests, low-level affiliation and the dreaded ECM (Electronic Counter-Measures). Up till now the longest I'd been strapped to a Phantom was two hours. Now I'd be facing a five hour fifteen minute transit through the Med with tanker support. Previously RAFG squadrons had staged to Cyprus via Italy and Greece. This time we were to use Victor tankers and deploy the whole squadron in one go. At the time (1981) the RAF had just one tanker aircraft, the Handley Page Victor. This single-tanker choice seemed foolhardy in the extreme. Had the Victor suffered the same fate as the Valiant and been grounded the RAF would have been without tankers of any shape. Of course twelve months later we would be at war in the Falkland Islands, and Vulcans, Hercules, VC10s and Tristars would all be quickly converted into tankers. For now we had the supremely reliable Victors. Still in their grey and green bomber camouflage, they were like no other aircraft flying at that time, with a massive tail, blisters above and below the wing and a cockpit that possessed little or no view, presumably a throwback from its nuclear role. They were, however, superb as airborne tankers. Always on time and always in the right place, they were the ultimate professionals doing a thankless task.

In order to arrive in Cyprus by 2 p.m. we had to leave Wildenrath at the ungodly hour of 5 a.m. Not being an operational station as such Akrotiri only opened from 7 in the morning till mid-afternoon. Briefing was fairly complex. Getting ten Phantoms from Germany to Cyprus in one go was not that simple. We'd be using a pair of our sister squadron's jets as spares. With an establishment of eleven aircraft the chances of having ten serviceable were slim. We learn the route in minute detail. The looser plan – how we'll cascade if aircraft go U/S on the ground, who has priority for spare aircraft – the list was endless. Then we brief the tanker join, and where we are going to rendezvous. Fortunately the tanker force has planned in detail how much fuel we'll have along our route. We are going in

Pairs take-offs were always good photo opportunities. Al Chubb tucks the gear up smartly in this freshly painted 19 Squadron Phantom.

groups of two, threes and a four. It's going to take a huge amount of coordination. Empty tankers will land in Sicily and full Victors will then get airborne to take us on to Cyprus. If we delay at any stage then we need to contact our Operations pronto. The last thing we want is to have the tankers airborne while we delay. As well as going into the finer points of aerial jousting our leader talks about diversions. If we can't take on fuel or have a technical problem where are we going to divert. Suitable runways along our trail are all identified. First choice is given to military airfields, particularly ones with arrestor cables in case we have hydraulic problems. Second choice is civilian airports with runways long enough to accept our military hardware. The Côte d'Azur is a favourite choice for obvious reasons.

Briefings over we walk in slow time to our allotted shelters. Weighed down with the baggage that goes with a 5-hour transit the journey to dispersal takes longer than normal. Most of the aircraft are carrying the baggage pod on the left wing. This allows us to carry enough clothes for an unscheduled overnight stop. The catering section have packed us up a 'goody box', most of which is inedible! Our start-up is uneventful and very soon we are lined up in echelon on the runway's end. Dawn is just visible through our misted Perspex canopies. With the cabin temperature set to warm we soon demist. I can imagine the noise as we blast off down the runway at this unearthly hour. As we snake upwards I lock our radar on to our leader; my pilot can see the twinkling of his navigation lights and closes up on him. I monitor carefully our closure rate and start my usual repertoire of elevation, angle-off and overtake. History has shown that these simple transit missions often end up being the most dangerous owing to their benign nature. We reach our cruising altitude and set course for France. In the blink of an eye we are soon crossing the Belgian border into France. As the sun slowly rises the city of Paris is clearly visible. Bathed in an ethereal mist the city looks surreal in the orange glow. As we pass overhead we ready ourselves for our first refuelling bracket. The French are particular that we perform our mid-air replenishment in the correct places. In the past they have been known to scramble fighters to observe the procedure.

The whole process of joining the tanker is complex in the extreme. In our Phantoms it's bread and butter stuff but it requires masses of discipline from all parties. By day it's pretty simple: find the tanker on radar, get the pilot's eyes on to the tanker then sit back. By night or in cloud it is an art to get 25 tons of Phantom travelling at 300 miles an hour within 300 yards of our flying gas station. Today the weather is perfect: clear skies and no turbulence. We get ourselves into formation and close up a thousand feet below our Victor. The sight of this converted bomber is more than welcome. If he had been delayed or was not in place we'd be looking at a diversion to a French air base. As we close on the tanker we run through our pre-refuelling checks. My driver selects the probe to out. The refuelling probe is beside my right shoulder and the noise of the door opening is startling. The airflow is disturbed as this large metal perch is pushed into the airflow. With our lance extended we're ready to take on fuel. I make sure the radar is off as we close up behind the basket. Trailing on a length of black rubber hose is the metal basket my pilot has to fly his probe into. As a backseater my job is either to try to talk the pilot in, or to shut up! On this occasion my pilot is seasoned enough to do his own thing. As we make contact there's a resounding clunk as the probe and basket lock. Instantly the lights ahead in the refuelling pod turn green indicating fuel flows. I'm acutely aware that gallons of aviation fuel are being pressure-fed down a pipe just inches from my head. I try not to think of the consequences of burst pipes or a stray spark causing a fire. We bob up and down in unison, attached by our umbilical cord. As the tanks fill up the lights turn amber and we need to disconnect. My pilot eases the throttles back and slowly we slide back, dropping out of contact. We can relax again, till the next bracket. All we have to do is follow the Victor tanker as he takes the lead. We track south past Sardinia then head for the toe of Italy. As we approach Sicily we bid farewell to our empty tanker as he heads for Palermo. His job is complete. He radioes ahead and the next tanker gets airborne from Palermo to start the whole process again. After our second tanking bracket we have enough gas to make it on to Cyprus on our own. Our two Speys spool up as we accelerate to Mach 9, leaving our gas station behind. I select the radar to map and ease the scanner down. The lazy sweep of the antenna nods down and starts to paint the sea. As I ease it up degree by degree the Cypriot coastline starts to appear, glowing an eerie green. As we approach the coast we start to move into echelon formation. After a 5-hour transit everyone is fatigued. . . .

An advance party in place and locals eager to see the real Air Force, we prepare to arrive in style. The landmarks unfamiliar to this first-time visitor, my seasoned pilot tries to give me a running commentary. As we get visual with the runway, the vast base of Akrotiri becomes apparent. In contrast to the usual RAF station this has none of the trappings of a Second World War airfield. It is baked dry, a brownish-yellow mix of sand and concrete. Large areas are devoted to giant solid structures, symbols of days gone by. Once the staging post en route to the Far East, this had been the RAF's finest hour, home to Vulcan bombers, Hercules transport and it's own dedicated fighter squadron – all now gone. My

This 92 Squadron F4 was one of the most brightly marked with its red fin and chequered RWR. It was photographed during a period when engineers ruled the RAF and adopted a bizarre two-letter tail code.

Perspex world turns from blue to metal as my pilot brings us in close to the other F4s. It's a surreal feeling sitting in the back of an F4 while someone else controls your destiny. As we claw round the peninsular, our speed pegged at 420 knots, we ease out into echelon starboard. It's an impressive sight, three camouflaged F4s and one grey all bouncing in unison, all dangerously close. I savour the moment as we hit the threshold. The leader breaks and I watch his aircraft stand on its side, belly streaked in oil, airbrakes out. I check around the cockpit for loose articles. After 5 hours stuck in this metal box the last thing I want is a sandwich to come flying at me as we rack on the 'G's. Over we go and my pilot's hands are a blur in the front. What with checking and re- checking airbrakes out, then in, flaps down, hook up, hydraulics good, fuel checked, it's a busy time. I glance out of the left quarter light, for me life is less pressed. I watch transfixed as our formation spreads out along the horizon and begins the slide towards the runway. No longer purposefully fighter, each Phantom looks like a wounded animal – flaps drooping, gear down, nose high, trailing smoke. We turn finals and point at the threshold – seconds later we arrive with a characteristic thump . . . good chute. As we reach the runway end the giant arrestor barrier raised to catch us drops down, no longer needed and as if to salute our arrival. As we turn clear our chute is jettisoned, onto the stony gravel. Simultaneously we crack canopies – the fresh air is welcome after a long transit. The stiff breeze brushes my cheeks as I unhook my oxygen mask. Two red weals score my cheeks; it's my longest flight in a fast jet to date.

The 2-mile taxi back to our dispersal is over quickly. We wave to our admirers at the tower and gaze at local workers digging with pickaxes. As we near the end of the taxi-way we turn right onto our dispersal and the old fighter line greets us. For once the Germany Phantoms are lined up with guardsman-like precision, all in a row. It's an impressive sight and a reminder of the 1960s, an era before concrete shelters. As we come on to chocks I tidy the rear cockpit and get ready to shut down the INAS. Ground crew swarm around us like white flies. By the end of the detachment their pale skins will be tanned a mixture of sun and oil. With a metallic chattering the twin speys wind down and we can dismount. No sooner have the engines wound down than the aircraft are being stripped. Off come the two Sgt Fletcher fuel tanks then the bulbous centreline tank. Having been cleaned, the Phantom looks the part. Sitting high on its undercarriage, wings bent up, tail dropped it looks every inch a fighter. No sooner have the engineers stripped it bare, they attach the deadly SU23 cannon under its belly, our whole purpose for being here. The last of the gun fighters is back.

Head throbbing from an overdose of brandy sours we arrive at the first briefing. For flyers the first day is always the worst on APC (Armament Practice Camp). Those of us who belong in the blue are faced by a sea of khaki. The Phantoms are being prepared for gun-fighting and for the aircrew we are due to be tortured by view foil. The list seems endless: gunnery theory, range safety orders, the gunnery pattern, talks on our banner towers – the Canberra Squadron. As if the operational side isn't bad enough, we are then given the 'Beano' brief. So-called after the comic strip, it's a list of dos and don'ts for visiting fighter squadrons – they'll Beano low flybys, Beano drinking off limits, etc. All of these rules are taken with a pinch of salt to any self-respecting fighter crew. On my first mission I find

Staying close at low level. No. 19 Squadron's liberally chequered aircraft were a stark contrast to the drab camouflage applied to the overland Phantoms.

out what all the fun is about. At the end of the westerly runway lies the entrance to this vast airbase and situated here is the RAF police picket post manned 24 hours a day. Although they do a sterling job, which is protecting our bases, they do tend to put the dampers on any squadron's high spirits and are therefore suitable for a spot of baiting. Everyday for five weeks we get airborne, clean up, leave the burners in and rotate just a few feet above the police post. The noise must be deafening but to us fighter jocks the joy is childish but amusing. Perhaps it's because of the constant dangers of flying Phantoms in the low-level air-defence role or perhaps it's the fighting spirit.

Briefings over, we settle down to the mundane chores of squadron life. Very early next morning we prepare for our first mission. To avoid the hottest part of the day we launch the first wave at 7 a.m. Our first brief is pretty lengthy, but by the end of the detachment it will be down to a couple of minutes. With this completed, we walk into the adjacent operations room to check what tail number we have and to chat with the engineers to see what snags we are carrying – nil defects, a good ship.

For our first cine sortie the gun is made safe. We have been allocated Phantom XV430, code letter C or Charlie. This aircraft is a bit of an odd ball as it was once a recce bird and is now the only Phantom on the squadron lacking the fin top RWR modification. It is also the dirtiest Phantom on strength; in fact it's probably the dirtiest Phantom in the RAF. It's one of the original light-grey F4s and is now showing its age. The paint is a very dull matt and every boot mark, scuff and oil streak has been etched onto the surface. It looks like a war machine. As we strap into the beast, beyond us is another sinister American product, the black dragon lady awaits her astronaut ready for the early push. We maintain strict radio silence so as not to compromise his clandestine mission. We watch in awe as the jet-black glider punches a hole in the early sky.

Speys turning, we check in with our tug the Canberra crew; all seems as planned and we taxi out behind English Electrics finest (save for the vertical twin jet!). Hooking up to the banner is a slow process and we sit burning gas needlessly. With a nod of the head our tug driver releases the brakes and pulls the banner cleanly into the sky. Smartly we take to the runway. Brakes on, power up, brakes off, burners in. The kick is a pleasant surprise after the heavy machine we normally fly. The nose lifts up making us look like a Navy F4 and we rotate. No sooner airborne than Andy tucks the gear up. He's still visual with the banner as I start the radar up. Lucky for me I'm flying with an old hand and he talks me onto the target. I move the scanner up and down far too quickly and miss the target. Andy calls me to look 1° up and BINGO, I can see two distinct blobs on the screen. Now I have to put my acquisition markers over the correct bleep and squeeze for a lock. Contrary to popular belief, squeezing the hand controller as hard as possible will not induce a lock! The trick now is to make sure we've locked onto the banner and not the Canberra. As we close up I give Andy a running commentary on range and overtake, ensuring we are not transferring lock to the target. With the weapon system checked we begin our cine pattern. Like weaving a rug, we subject our F4 to lots of 'G' for 45 minutes – we must do about ten passes and by the end I'm getting tired. Although we aren't carrying live ammunition, we call switches safe and head for base. With a clean-wing Phantom and 5 minutes of spare fuel Andy does a couple of aerobatic manoeuvres in the Cyprus blue. My world turns blue then brown then blue. After a long cine session it's just what I need.

Mission over we head for the camera debrief. Our squadron weapons instructor looks at the film, all 10 minutes of it frame by frame. I sit at

Shooting into sun is not normally the best way of taking photographs but this unusual shot accentuates the setting sun and the magnificently aggressive shape of the Phantom.

the back trying to fathom out what's going on. Grainy black-and-white images all in negative are hard to grasp at first. All I can tell is the angle off is pretty good (inside 15° and the tug pilot gets worried) and the ranges look good. Film critique complete, we get the all clear – one more cine and we'll be firing hot. The formalities of the second cine over, we launch for our first hot sortie. The aim is to achieve at least a 15% average twice in six sorties. In our first attempt we achieve a creditable 26% and on our next an even better 37%. For us the heat is off as we are 'Ace' qualified; for others the process will take longer, for some much longer.

With the excellent weather factor we fly twice a day and I continue my squadron conversion. With the aircraft in the clean wing fit, supersonic intercepts are easy to achieve. Despite what the books say, getting the RAF Phantom to Mach 2 is not straightforward. We do however settle for second best and see 1,000 knots on the inertial ground-speed read out. For a backseater, supersonic intercepts are really a test of your metal. With a split range of 50 miles two Phantoms closing together at 2,000 knots will pass beak to beak in about 2 minutes. A 10° error on heading will put you miles off course in the blink of an eye, a fumbled attempt at a radar lock will almost certainly deny you a radar missile shot. Coupled with all this, your two thirsty speys are spitting out fuel faster than you can register on the fuel gauge. If you screw up it's unlikely there will be a re-run, this is a one-shot manoeuvre. Luckily for me I'm blessed with a good radar, which holds its lock and allows us to dispatch our target to a simulated watery grave.

All too quickly our squadron's month-long spell in the sun is over and we return to the murk of the North German plain. However, life on the Germany Phantom Squadrons was never dull. The exercises seemed relentless – station exercises, Maxevals, Minevals and Tacevals. All meaningless names for playing war games. Often we'd spend days wandering from shelter to shelter, gas mask in hand, launching off on another 2ATAF SOP's (2nd Allied Tactical Air Force Standard Operating Procedures) sortie. These were halcyon days of cruising around at low level at 420 knots looking to pick a fight with anyone who got in the way. Often the affiliation exercise would be pre-booked Jaguars from nearby Bruggen or Buccaneers from Laarbruch, difficult opponents. Equally hard to fight were the diminutive Harrier GR3s from Gutersloh. Working closely with our NATO allies Phantoms would often join other fighters on cap. During the 1980s Europe turned F16, the Dutch and Belgians being favoured partners. With our superior AWG12 radar the RAF Phantoms could pick up low-altitude targets at far greater range than the agile fighters. With our two-man crew it's also much easier to run the intercept.

Due to the nature of our low-level air-defence role the Wildenrath wing was essentially a day fighter force. Night flying was a fairly rare event, with most of it performed over central Germany at medium level. We assumed that as the Warsaw Pact forces at that time had no real low-level night-attack capability we would only be facing a medium-level threat. In fact most of our medium-level flying was geared to honing our skills for battle flight duties. This involved intercepting high-flying or slow-speed targets and then creeping up behind them to within a couple of hundred yards, all to identify rather than engage.

As well as the annual APC there was also the annual MPC (Missile Practice Camp). Each air-defence squadron would be allocated a number of missiles to fire during a two-week period while based at RAF Valley on Holyhead Island in Wales. Normally 19 Squadron was allocated the two-week slot in February each year, not renowned as having the best weather factor. Crews would be picked well in advance in order that each pilot and navigator fired one missile during their three-year tour. Engineers would also begin preparations well before the annual deployment. Where possible the RAF had a policy that each aircraft should fire various missiles during its career. This gave the crews confidence in the weapon system in each aircraft. This theory was put to the test when 92 Squadron Phantom XV422 accidentally shot down a 31 Squadron Jaguar on 25 May 1982. While the ground crew prepared the aircraft for weapon release, crews flew their allocated profiles first in the simulator then in the air. With many eyes watching each missile launch this was not the place to make a mistake. Normally the squadron deployed five Phantoms allowing us to fly four-ship missions with a spare aircraft. Weather was always a major factor in determining your stay at Holyhead. Often the task of firing a handful of missles could be accomplished in about a week. As 19 Squadron were blessed with the winter period it was nearly always the full two weeks.

In Germany on the Phantom crews averaged about 220 hours per year on type, or a little over 20 hours a month. Air and ground crews were always fiercely proud to be serving on a front-line Phantom squadron. The mere sight of a fully tooled up FGR2 evoked a mixture of fear and pride in squadron members. If it came to conflict every one knew that although not the newest machine, the Phantom would come up with the goods. The premature demise of the Germany Phantoms left the RAF with just one fighter type, the vapid Tornado F3. Although it would have been an adequate replacement for the Phantom, it would never possess the sheer aggression and raw power of the mighty F4.

CHAPTER 9

Time We Were Leaving

Pat Watling

It was 3 June 1980 and Sid and I had just completed our second one-versus-one combat mission against a USAF (Europe) F5 belonging to the elite 525th Aggressor Squadron based at RAF Alconbury. We had learnt a few lessons from our previous sortie and had some encouraging success in our ageing Phantom FG1 against such a challenging adversary. Our fuel state had dictated that we end our fight so we 'bugged out', having explored a wide range of energy states and G levels during our encounter. Our return to Alconbury was uneventful. We joined the visual circuit, performing a run and break just to put our aircraft and bodies through a final work-out before landing.

The finals turn went fine and we completed our landing checks, reducing power to slow back to 132 knots. Sid (Steve James), being a considerate navigator, called 300 feet as we were operating unusually on airfield QNH. At that time the RAF operated on QFE. Very soon after his utterance, and to my great surprise, the nose of the aircraft rapidly disappeared from view ahead of me as it swung around to appear out of my right windscreen, pointing rearwards. Initial incredulity was soon followed by two very restrained comments. Sid said 'Blimey!' and I said 'Och no!' – after all I had been living in Scotland for a while. This emergency had never been covered in the simulator, and so there were no immediate action drills.

The initial effect of this airframe rearrangement was to start the aircraft rolling slowly to the right. At just 5 knots above landing speed my options were limited as it was very inadvisable to use large inputs of aileron at such an angle of attack in the F4, as the aircraft is likely to flick in the opposite direction. I therefore applied a bootful of left rudder and a small amount of left aileron in an attempt to correct our flight path in roll at least. We were still descending so I started to increase power but, although no obvious warning clangers had gone off, my gaze hadn't been able to absorb what looked like an oversized ice-cream cone stuck in the right intake.

I was quickly aware that the scenario required a rapid decision as any further descent and roll would have reduced our chances of a survivable ejection. I guess around 4 or 5 seconds passed while I tried to resolve the problem, but then I concluded that becoming a statistic was not an attractive option. I decided to eject soon after. Two thoughts entered my mind before I pulled the bottom handle. First, I had a substantial

XT870
S
3

Previous page: Every couple of months Leuchars-based FG1s would perform 'ranger' exercises. Normally a pair of FG1s would fly to Wildenrath for a weekend stop-over. Occasionally they would return on the Monday, having sampled a 2ATAF low-level mission in the morning.

amount of left rudder applied and I had vowed to myself that should the need ever arise I would eject with the rudders central, if I could. A colleague had received serious leg injuries after leaving a Lightning with 'asymmetric legs'. However, centralising the rudder would have increased the roll rate, making matters worse. Second, Sid's wife was pregnant; I don't know why I thought of that one!

There was no time to tell Sid to go. He would soon get the drift when he saw my size 9s leaving vertically atop a burning rocket plume. Our procedures dictated that, if time was short, the pilot should leave first. Command ejection seats were not in service at that time. I imagined that the delay between pulling the handle and actually launching up the seat rails would seem interminable but was pleasantly surprised. Having made the effort to force my head back against the headrest I next saw the rocket pack ignite below my seat, thus saving the forward tuck that I never quite managed in the gym at school.

I was next aware of the quiet and almost eerie world that I had been beamed up into and that the backs of my legs were a bit the worse for wear. I had trained regularly in the drills required following such an event, but on the day my recall of them was scant. I first decided to lower my oxygen mask, as I could no longer breathe. I decided not to remove the pins from the Kosch fasteners of my harness. One wrong move and I would have lost the parachute. It had happened before. It was too late to release the survival pack from underneath my rear as the ground was coming up too fast. I adopted the so-called 'parachute posture' but was in two minds whether to relax or maintain a rigid posture. I therefore did neither and the result was like jumping off a 15-foot brick wall. Side right or left was good in theory but my parachute was not of the sporting variety and so landing in a crumpled heap seemed more appropriate. As I lay there, relieved that the Martin Baker seat had just saved my life, I elected to wiggle my limbs before leaping to my feet and possibly doing some serious damage. While doing so I heard a sort of loud low rumbling sound. As it got louder I worked out that I had landed quite close to the main London to Scotland railway line. A high-speed train rushed past, close enough to deflate my 'chute.

As I stood up I spotted Sid, who had dusted himself down and repacked his 'chute. As I walked towards him across the smouldering scar that the Phantom had carved across the field I found a liquid oxygen bottle, which I elected to kick for no apparent reason. As we met up I noticed that Sid no longer had his left eyebrow or eyelashes – my rocket seat had burnt them off during my exit.

We were greeted by what appeared to be a bionic American firefighter bounding towards us at high speed in a silver suit. He asked if we were OK and did we know where the other pilot had landed? It seemed unlikely that our adversary had followed our footsteps and crashed behind us. He hadn't, and once he had established that we were both alive transmitted 'Oh well, a kill's a kill!' A cheap shot indeed.

The Phantom in question, FG1 XV589, had been an ex-Fleet Air Arm aircraft. Retired from naval use in late 1979 it was modified and issued to the RAF some months before its fateful sortie. It was one of the first aircraft to be painted in the new grey scheme. It was lost because the radome catch failed. After years of use on ship with the radome being opened and closed regularly the catch had become worn and it had failed at a critical moment. Other Phantoms were found to be suffering the same defect.

CHAPTER 10

Phantom Display Pilot

Archie Liggat

Running through his pre-flight checks, a Phantom pilot of 56 Squadron prepares for an overseas mission. Air defence crews tended to wear white helmets to reflect the heat at altitude.

Previous page: Stripped of its stores the F4 was a surprisingly agile fighter for its age. Running in for a flypast over Venice airport, Paul Willis holds station on the lead Phantom in August 1983.

Mark 'Manners' Manwaring and I had been chosen to provide the public with the last ever solo aerobatics display by the unique and venerable Phantom. As the aircraft were to be scrapped, we were unusually permitted to explore the boundaries of the flight envelope to ensure a 'phitting phinale'. We were then relative youngsters but our mount was not and she showed her displeasure at our gusto by shedding bits of herself on more than one occasion. What follows is the story of one such event.

In May I had foolishly burst a tyre in front of the crowd at the North Weald show while attempting not to go off the end of their short rough little runway. We had also dropped a refuelling probe door into a field near Mildenhall during their annual air show. In doing so I had bent more of the queen's metal than I had done in the previous twelve years – apart from these two incidents all had gone well.

It was now 25 July 1992 and we were well into the season with over twenty displays in the bag. We were flying twin-sticker XT914, returning from Leeming as a pair with reserve jet XV393 for the last public display at our home base, RAF Wattisham, before its closure. As luck would have it both aircraft were unserviceable for display so Manners passed a message to Wattisham via Air Traffic to prepare a jet, any jet, for the vital event. Once on the ground we were confronted with single-sticker XV465. Both the display jets were purposely dual-control variants. This made us feel much better as Manners had some instruments in the back allowing us to cross-check gate heights, speeds and pitch angles and so on. Both display aircraft also sported newly manufactured outer wing panels and enjoyed unique servicing checks jealously carried out by a dedicated, eagle-eyed team of engineers led by Nev Gardner. Meanwhile single-sticker XV465 squatted apologetically on the tarmac, ailerons drooping, dripping oil slightly and staring into the distance, as if feeling guilty for offering nothing special.

Display flying for front-line crews was a fairly rare event with so many operational commitments.

The 92 Squadron blue Phantom, photographed from the top of a refuelling bowser at RAF Leeming just weeks before the Phantom was withdrawn from RAF service.

Tail-end view of a 56 Squadron FGR2 with everything dangling. Below the rudder the 'fish-tail' opening a fuel-venting outlet. Fuel dumping was from the wings between the flaps and ailerons.

Diamond 9 from 56 Squadron.

Aerobatic teams spend many hours practising close formations. Fighter squadrons normally fly big formations once a year with no practice. Here 19 Squadron put an Echelon 9 with a mix of grey and grey-green machines in July 1982.

Bristling with weapons, the Phantom was the first truly multi-role jet fighter. It excelled at both air-to-ground and air-to-air combat. John Allison is seen here over a grey German cloud scene.

There was no time for sentiment – our display slot was in 15 minutes! Attach jet to body, wind her up . . . functionals . . . and off I go straight into the full looping show as it's such a beautiful day. Aware of the critical eye of wife, child, public and colleagues, I want this to be a good one. Manners sits grunting in the back seat, denied much of his normal patter, glumly enduring repeated G-snatches and max roll rates.

. . . Zero pitch rate, full aileron roll (the Phantom is inclined to inertial cross-coupling), and check inverted – pause two three, Roll! (heads bounce off canopy), check pull! 8G sustained: huge grunting to stop greying out, over

High over the Cypriot hills, Mike Roe skirts the coastline inbound to RAF Akrotiri.

No. 92 Squadron's twin-sticker receives the full 19 Squadron treatment during a visit to Cyprus.

Producing an image like this is as much down to the skills of the chase pilot as to the photographer. Barrel rolling over a large formation at close proximity requires a lot of skill. It also needs to be done as slowly and smoothly as possible or the picture will be a blur. Here are six FGR2s of 56 (Firebird) Squadron in plan form.

the top (line, gate height, check speed) pull through and commit . . . The jet feels unfamiliar but OK: a bit loose but in a rumbly sort of way.

. . . 6G snatch to base, rad alt skips on 500 feet burner shunt . . . crowd centre, PULL! Oxygen mask tears at face, snatch a breath and strain against the pain and peripheral grey as the body surrenders to the crushing constriction of the G-suit. Inverted, grass and runway above, pink faces looking up, I'm blinking against the dust from the cockpit floor. Slow up . . . relief. On line and everything out for the dirty barrel role: pitch up, hold the donut (Optimum 19 AOA), stick central and delicate roll with rudder – don't rely on aileron – rudder interconnect with flaps this time. Clean up on the way round. Final full burner 690 knots pass at 100 feet and massive pull into the vertical sees us as a snowball through 25,000 feet in 25 seconds! Being 5 tons lighter than 6 minutes before, it's time to land.

Breaking out. As soon as you were airborne as a close pair it was normal procedure to split away into tactical formation.

Overleaf: Waiting for clearance. A pair of Phantoms about to launch against a pair of Lightnings on a dissimilar air combat sortie.

November 1981 and Reg Hallam prepares to fight the F15 Eagles of the Bitburg Wing. The Italian air base at Decimomannu in Sardinia for the ACMI (Air Combat Manoeuvring and Instrumentation range) was a popular destination for RAF fighters.

Flyers and fixers. A joint 19/92 Squadron detachment to the Belgian Air Force base at Beauvachain. Smiles reflect the high morale on the Phantom fleet.

AA
F

Mission accomplished. XV439 taxies back to the ramp surrounded by ground equipment and personnel. As on aircraft carriers, flight lines are busy and dangerous places. At the back of the Phantom the clamshell door is open; this is where the brake parachute is normally housed.

Mick Mercer, oxygen mask removed, smiles for the camera. The aircraft is in an unusual configuration. On the rear station is a live Skyflash missile. On the outboard wing is a Bullpup missile-turned-camera. On the forward station is a strike camera used by the recce Phantoms. The aircraft is shown just before a live missile firing, hence the unusual fit.

A 23 Squadron Red Eagles Phantom awaits its crew. Hung on the pilot's ladder is the combined harness originally used by Phantom crews to attach themselves to the Martin Baker seats.

'Good Chute' – Andy Lister Tomlinson checks the rear-view mirror and confirms to the pilot that the 'chute is deployed.

'Black Mike.' One of the most famous RAF Phantom FG1s was this 111 Squadron machine. Still preserved by the squadron, the aircraft is lovingly looked after.

XT911 (K) was 19 Squadron's only dual-control Phantom and as such was normally flown with a pilot in the back seat performing check rides on other squadron pilots.

We broke into the circuit and plonked on to the ground 2 minutes later. Chute jettisoned, pins in, canopy open (blessed relief) we taxied sedately off the runway and nodded politely to the assembled crowd at the nearby boundary fence. They seemed very enthusiastic – even agitated – and seemed to be brandishing curiously familiar pieces of twisted metal painted air defence grey! I began to feel uneasy. Manners noticed too. One of the tyres had a flat spot and we bumped our way back to dispersal, our elation replaced by a growing sense of foreboding.

It seems the whole base was there to meet us, including the Station Commander and Officer Commanding Engineering Wing. Some ground-crew were pointing incredulously at the starboard wing (which can't be seen from the cockpit). We shut down and clambered out under the frown of higher authority. It would be wrong to say that most of the wing tip had vanished – but not that wrong. It was as if a great white shark had taken a bite out of the trailing edge. Tattered honey-comb metal hung down forlornly. Devoid of aileron and with leading edge flaps still working, we had been unaware that the wing tip had shredded at some point during the display. The tower had noticed our loss during final approach, but the horrified public had seen it immediately.

Running in for the break a pair of F4s hold 420 knots at 1,500 feet. Despite its recent grey repaint the nearest aircraft (XV400) is already showing signs of wear.

Seen at Akrotiri in August 1990 is 'C' of 19 Squadron, deployed as part of the build-up in the Gulf ahead of Operation Granby.

Shark-mouthed XV481 at Corsica.

Plan view of live-armed XV437.

John Allison and Jack Thomson blast off Wildenrath's rain-soaked runway, 1983. Jack sadly lost his life in the back seat of a Phantom during practice for the Abingdon air show.

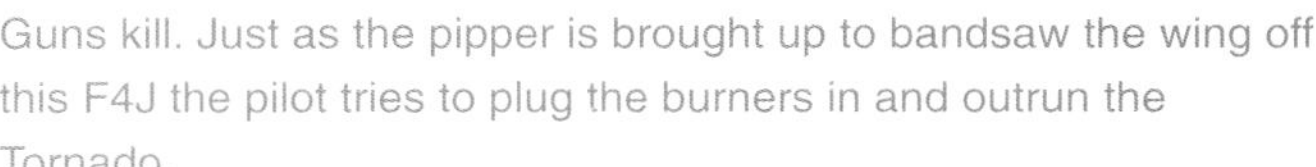

Guns kill. Just as the pipper is brought up to bandsaw the wing off this F4J the pilot tries to plug the burners in and outrun the Tornado.

RAF Germany in the 1980s at the height of the Cold War. Bloodhound missiles point east, ready to engage any threat.

Echelon 9. At the end of a long armament practice camp it was decided to put all ten of the squadron's Phantoms in the air. After a few flypasts in Diamond 9 formation an echelon was formed off the coast.

Rain or shine Phantoms ripped through the sky for almost a quarter of a century in RAF service.

A thorough search failed to recover many of the bits. The breeze had carried the honeycomb interior and light outer skin towards the jubilant crowd on the airfield boundary, presumably to be carried away as cherished booty. No doubt even today pieces lie in the hands of ardent enthusiasts. Bad press followed. Our grim history of structural failure was photographically revealed to the world. 'Experts' extolled the dangers of flying with an incomplete airframe but by then we were getting used to it.

We 'held it together', as they say, for the remaining twenty-five shows, culminating in the final Phantom display at RAF Leuchars on 19 September 1992. The Phantom was, and for some air forces still is, a mighty fighter: capable beyond its years and thoroughly dependable, able to shrug off the sort of inadvertent amputations that might prove disastrous for its more highly strung electronic successors. A victory of brute force over aerodynamics, it exuded personality, spoke to those who would listen and demanded to be taken seriously by pilots and adversaries alike.

'Shine on you crazy Phantom' – with apologies to Pink Floyd!

A Cobra Phantom over a typical German backdrop.

Main picture: Once lovingly cared for and now reduced to scrap the 111 Squadron FG1 flagship XV574 awaits the cutter's torch at the Wattisham dump.

Such was the thrust of a Spey-powered clean-wing Phantom that rotation and gear retraction were almost one action. John Cliffe gets XV497 off the Deci concrete.

Glossary of Terms and Abbreviations

ADI	Attitude Direction Indicator
ADIZ	Air Defence Interception Zone
AOA	Angle of Attack
ATAF	Allied Tactical Air Force
BDRT	Battle Damage Repair Training
Bleed air	Hot engine air bled over the wings
Boundary layer	Hot air
FIPZ	Fighter Interception Protection Zone
HAS	Hardened Aircraft Shelters
HE	High Explosive
HSI	Horizontal Situation Indicator
INAS	Inertial Navigation and Attack System
Maxevals	Maximum Evaluations
Phandet	Phantom detachment
QFE	Pressure altitude above the airfield
QNH	Pressure above sea level
QRA	Quick Reaction Alert
RHAG	Rotary Hydraulic Arrestor Gear
RWR	Radar Warning Receiver
Stabilator	Phantom elevator
Tacan	Tactical Air Navigation System
Tacevals	Tactical Evaluations
VASI	Visual Approach Slope Indicator

Down but not out: a 74 Squadron Phantom flies alongside the author's Tornado just a few days before disbandment.

Appendices

Key

A/C	Aircraft
BDRT	Battle Damage Repair Training
GI	Ground Instructional
LU	RAF Leuchars
Watt	RAF Wattisham
W/O	Written Off

I – FG1 Fates

XT595	Scrapped cockpit section used by RAF exhibition flight
XT596	Preserved at Fleet Air Arm Museum
XT597	Preserved at Boscombe Down
XT598	W/O 23/11/78 111 Sqn
XT857	Became 8913M GI A/C 9/86; scrapped LU 4/92
XT858	Fatigue test aircraft at BAE Brough; scrapped 1994
XT859	Scrapped LU 4/92
XT860	W/O 20/04/88 43 Sqn Transatlantic air race winner
XT861	W/O 07/09/87 111 Sqn
XT862	W/O 19/05/71 RN
XT863	Nose preserved 2001; scrapped 1992 at Abingdon
XT864	LU BDR 8998M
XT865	Scrapped Watt 9/91
XT866	W/O 09/07/81 43 Sqn
XT867	LU BDR 9064M; scrapped by July 2001
XT868	W/O 12/05/78 RN
XT869	W/O 03/12/74 RN
XT870	Scrapped 4/92
XT871	W/O 8/11/74 RN
XT872	Scrapped Watt 9/91
XT873	Scrapped Watt 9/91
XT874	Scrapped 4/92
XT875	Scrapped Watt 9/91
XT876	W/O 10/01/72 RN
XV565	W/O 29/06/71 RN
XV566	W/O 03/05/70 RN
XV567	Scrapped LU 4/92
XV568	Scrapped LU 4/92
XV569	Bruggen 9063M
XV570	Scrapped Watt 9/92
XV571	Scrapped LU 3/92 43 Sqn flagship
XV572	Scrapped LU 4/92
XV573	Scrapped LU 4/92
XV574	Scrapped Watt 1991 111 Sqn flagship
XV575	Scrapped Watt 9/91
XV576	Scrapped Watt 9/91
XV577	LU BDR 9065M; scrapped by 4/2001
XV578	W/O 28/02/79 111 Sqn
XV579	Scrapped LU 4/92
XV580	W/O 18/09/75 43 Sqn
XV581	Nose at 2489 Sqn ATC Aberdeen
XV582	LU BDR Black Mike, preserved 111 Sqn current September 2002
XV583	Scrapped Watt 9/91
XV584	Scrapped Watt 9/91
XV585	Scrapped LU 1995
XV586	LU BDR preserved
XV587	Scrapped Watt 4/93
XV588	W/O 13/05/77 RN
XV589	W/O 3/06/80 111 Sqn
XV590	Scrapped LU 4/92
XV591	Nose preserved at RAF Cosford;

scrapped owing to structural fault in 1987
XV592 Scrapped Watt 9/91

Total FG1s lost: 15

II – FGR2 FATES

Twin-stickers
XT852 West Freugh fire section
XT853 Scampton fire section; scrapped 10/95

XT891 Preserved RAF Coningsby
XT892 Scrapped Watt 4/93
XT893 W/O 24/04/89 56 Sqn
XT894 Scrapped Watt 9/92
XT895 RAF Valley fire section; scrapped by 9/92
XT896 Scrapped 27MU 8/95
XT897 Scrapped 27MU 8/95
XT898 RAF St Athan fire section; scrapped 1993
XT899 Preseved in Czech museum at Kbely
XT900 RAF Honnington 9099M; scrapped by 1995
XT901 Scrapped Watt 9/92
XT902 Scrapped Watt 9/92
XT903 Nose preserved at RAF Wyton
XT904 W/O 15/10/71 228 OCU
XT905 Preserved at North Luffenham
XT906 Scrapped Watt 6/93
XT907 Preserved as 9151M Chattenden
XT908 W/O 09/01/89 228 OCU
XT909 Scrapped Watt 9/92
XT910 Scrapped 27MU 8/95
XT911 Scrapped 9/95
XT912 W/O 14/04/82 in mid-air collision, 228 OCU
XT913 W/O 14/02/72 228 OCU
XT914 Preserved at RAF Brampton
XV393 Scrapped RAF Marham 9/94
XV394 Scrapped RAF Wildenrath 9/91 (damaged beyond repair)
XV395 W/O 09/06/69 228 OCU
XV396 Scrapped Watt 9/92
XV397 W/O 01/07/73 17 Sqn
XV398 Scrapped Watt 9/92
XV399 Nose preserved (no details); scrapped at St Athan 9/92
XV400 Scrapped Watt 9/91
XV401 Preserved at Boscombe Down 74 Sqn
XV402 Scrapped 1995
XV403 W/O 4/8/78 111 Sqn
XV404 Scrapped 1994
XV405 W/O 24/11/75 228 OCU
XV406 Preserved at Carlisle as 9098M
XV407 Fire training RAF Manston; burnt by 2001
XV408 Preserved at RAF Halton
XV409 Preserved at RAF Mount Pleasant
XV410 Scrapped Watt 9/92
XV411 Burnt at RAF Manston as 9103M
XV412 Laarbruch
XV413 W/O 12/11/80 29 Sqn
XV414 W/O 09/12/80 23 Sqn
XV415 Preserved at RAF Boulmer
XV416 W/O 03/03/75 111 Sqn
XV417 W/O 23/07/76 29 Sqn
XV418 W/O 11/07/80 92 Sqn
XV419 Scrapped Watt 6/93
XV420 Preserved at RAF Neatishead
XV421 W/O 10/91 1435 Flt Falkland Islands
XV422 Preserved at Stornoway but scrapped by 1998
XV423 Decoy at RAF Leeming; scrapped by July 2001
XV424 RAF Museum 9152M
XV425 Decoy at RAF Bruggen 9094M
XV426 Scrapped; parts at RAF Coltishall for BDRT then Coningsby
XV427 W/O 22/08/73 17 Sqn

XV428 W/O 23/09/88 228 OCU
XV429 Scrapped Watt 9/91
XV430 Watt fire section; scrapped by 3/92
XV431 W/O 11/10/74 31 Sqn
XV432 Scrapped Watt 9/92
XV433 Scrapped 27MU 8/95
XV434 W/O 07/01/86 29 Sqn
XV435 Llandbedr fire section
XV436 W/O 05/03/80 29 Sqn
XV437 W/O 18/10/88 92 Sqn
XV438 Scrapped Watt 9/92
XV439 Scrapped Watt 9/92
XV440 W/O 25/06/73 31 Sqn
XV441 W/O 21/11/74 14 Sqn
XV442 Scrapped Falkland Islands 8/92

XV460 Nose preserved
XV461 Scrapped Falkland Islands 8/92
XV462 W/O 8/1/91 19 Sqn
XV463 W/O 17/12/75 41 Sqn
XV464 Scrapped Watt 9/92
XV465 BDR Leeming; scrapped by 19 July 2001
XV466 Scrapped Falkland Islands 8/92
XV467 Preserved at Boulmer; scrapped 9/00
XV468 Preserved at Woodvale; scrapped by 2001
XV469 Scrapped 8/95
XV470 Preserved at RAF Akrotiri, Cyprus
XV471 W/O 3/7/86 19 Sqn
XV472 Scrapped Falkland Islands 8/92
XV473 Scrapped RAF Waddington
XV474 Preserved at Duxford
XV475 Bruggen
XV476 Scrapped Wattisham 9/92
XV477 W/O 6 Sqn 20/10/72
XV478 Damaged then scrapped at RAF Wildenrath by 1991
XV479 W/O 12/10/71 54 Sqn
XV480 Scrapped Watt 9/91
XV481 Bruggen
XV482 Scrapped LU 1995
XV483 W/O 24/7/78 92 Sqn
XV484 W/O Falkland Islands 17/10/83
XV485 Bruggen
XV486 Scrapped St Athan 1993
XV487 Scrapped 27MU 8/95
XV488 Scrapped Watt 9/92
XV489 Scrapped St Athan
XV490 Nose preserved; scrapped Watt 9/92
XV491 W/O 7/7/82 29 Sqn
XV492 Scrapped Watt 3/92
XV493 W/O 9/8/74 in mid-air collision with civilian aircraft; 41 Sqn
XV494 Scrapped Watt 9/92
XV495 Scrapped St Athan 1993
XV496 Scrapped Watt 6/93
XV497 RAF Coninsgby BDRT
XV498 Scrapped Watt 3/92
XV499 BDR Leeming; earmarked for Yorkshire Air Museum
XV500 Preserved at St Athan, painted as XV498
XV501 W/O France 56 Sqn

III – F4J FATES

ZE350 Pendine range parts preserved
ZE351 Scrapped RAF Finningly 11/95
ZE352 Pendine range parts preserved
ZE353 RAF Manston fire-fighting school; scrapped by 2001
ZE354 Coningsby BDR; scrapped
ZE355 Pendine range
ZE356 Waddington decoy BDRT
ZE357 Delivered to Bruggen for BDRT
ZE358 Crashed in South Wales
ZE359 Duxford Imperial War Museum, preserved as ex-US Navy F4J
ZE360 RAF Manston
ZE361 RAF Honnington; scrapped by December 2000
ZE362 Pendine range
ZE363 Pendine range

ZE350–ZE364 ex US Navy 153768, 152773, 153783, 153785, 153795, 153803, 153850, 153809, 155510, 155529, 155734, 155755, 155868, 155894

Some of the airframes that were sent as targets to ranges were in part later preserved as nose sections.

IV – RAF Phantom Squadron Histories

2(AC) Squadron
Base: RAF Laarbruch
Formed: 1 April 1976
Disbanded: February 1976
Aircraft used by Squadron: XT898, 901, 903, 906, 910; XV399, 411, 413, 417, 430, 439, 441, 464, 467, 468, 469, 470, 473, 474, 475, 485, 486, 488, 489, 494, 498

6 Squadron
Base: RAF Coningsby
Formed: 16 January 1969
Disbanded: 30 September 1974
Aircraft used by Squadron: XT892, 896, 899, 908; XV395, 399, 400, 403, 408, 413, 418, 420, 422, 423, 424, 425, 429, 432, 438, 442, 466, 477, 480, 481, 482, 490, 492, 495, 499

14 Squadron
Base: RAF Bruggen
Formed: 1 July 1970
Disbanded: 1 December 1975
Aircraft used by Squadron: XT900, 912, 914; XV411, 413, 417, 419, 421, 425, 432, 434, 435, 439, 441, 460, 463, 464, 466, 470, 473, 484, 485, 486, 496, 501

17(F) Squadron
Base: RAF Bruggen
Formed: 1 September 1970
Disbanded: February 1976
Aircraft used by Squadron: XT893, 894, 901, 905, 906; XV393, 397, 398, 425, 427, 428, 462, 468, 469, 470, 471, 474, 475, 483, 487, 488, 489, 494, 496, 497, 498

19(F) Squadron
Base: RAF Wildenrath
Formed: 1 October 1976
Disbanded: 9 January 1992
Aircraft used by Squadron: XT896, 898, 899, 901, 902, 908, 909, 911; XV396, 400, 401, 404, 407, 408, 411, 418, 419, 420, 421, 422, 428, 434, 437, 439, 460, 462, 464, 465, 467, 468, 469, 470, 471, 472, 474, 475, 476, 478, 480, 481, 484, 485, 487, 488, 491, 494, 496, 497, 498, 499

23 Squadron
Base: RAF Coningsby, Wattisham, Stanley, Mount Pleasant
Formed: 6 October 1975
Disbanded: 30 October 1988
Aircraft used by Squadron: XT899, 908, 909, 912; XV401, 402, 403, 404, 406, 408, 414, 415, 419, 420, 421, 422, 423, 425, 426, 430, 432, 434, 435, 437, 438, 442, 464, 465, 466, 472, 474, 476, 478, 481, 483, 484, 485, 486, 489, 490, 492, 494, 495, 496, 497, 499, 500

29(F) Squadron
Base: RAF Coningsby
Formed: 1 October 1974
Disbanded: 31 March 1987
Aircraft used by Squadron: XT894, 896, 898, 899, 902, 906, 909, 910, 912; XV399, 400, 401, 402, 404, 406, 407, 408, 409, 412, 413, 417, 418, 419, 420, 421, 423, 424, 425, 428, 429, 432, 433, 434, 436, 438, 442, 460, 461, 465, 466, 468, 471, 472, 473, 478, 481, 482, 484, 485, 486, 487, 488, 489, 490, 491, 492, 494, 495, 499, 500, 501

31 Squadron
Base: RAF Bruggen
Formed: 20 July 1971
Disbanded: 1 July 1976
Aircraft used by Squadron: XT900, 905, 906; XV393, 399, 402, 404, 415, 422, 426, 427, 431, 433, 434, 436, 440, 460, 462, 465, 474, 476, 480, 483, 484, 486, 487, 488, 491, 494, 501

41(F) Squadron
Base: RAF Coningsby
Formed: 1 April 1972
Disbanded: 31 March 1977
Aircraft used by Squadron: XV399, 400, 401, 402, 407, 409, 412, 413, 414, 418, 432, 434, 442, 462, 463, 465, 466, 471, 478, 480, 481, 483, 490, 492, 493, 495, 496, 497, 499

43(F) Squadron
Base: RAF Leuchars
Formed: 1 September 1969
Disbanded: 31 July 1989
Aircraft used by Squadron: XT860, 861, 863, 866, 873, 874, 875; XV406, 470, 489, 567, 568, 569, 571, 572, 573, 574, 575, 576, 577, 578, 579, 580, 581, 582, 583, 584, 585, 586, 587, 590

54 Squadron
Base: RAF Coningsby
Formed: 1 September 1969
Disbanded: 23 April 1974
Aircraft used by Squadron: XT891, 902; XV400, 403, 404, 406, 412, 414, 415, 416, 419, 420, 424, 429, 432, 434, 437, 461, 465, 478, 479, 482, 490, 495, 500

56(F) Squadron
Base: RAF Coningsby/Wattisham
Formed: July 1976
Disbanded: 1 July 1992
Aircraft used by Squadron: XT891, 892, 893, 894, 897, 899, 900, 901, 903, 906, 907, 908, 909, 910, 914; XV396, 399, 400, 401, 402, 404, 407, 409, 410, 411, 415, 420, 422, 423, 424, 425, 426, 428, 429, 432, 433, 434, 437, 438, 442, 460, 461, 464, 466, 467, 468, 469, 470, 472, 473, 474, 475, 476, 478, 480, 481, 482, 486, 487, 488, 489, 490, 492, 494, 495, 496, 497, 500, 501

64 Squadron/228 OCU
Base: RAF Coningsby/Leuchars
Formed: February 1968
Disbanded: 31 January 1991
Aircraft used by Squadron: XT891, 892, 893, 894, 895, 896, 897, 898, 899, 900, 901, 902, 903, 904, 905, 906, 907, 908, 909, 910, 911, 912, 913, 914; XV393, 394, 395, 396, 398, 399, 400, 401, 402, 404, 405, 406, 407, 408, 409, 410, 411, 412, 413, 415, 419, 421, 423, 424, 425, 426, 428, 429, 430, 432, 433, 434, 435, 436, 438, 442, 461, 462, 463, 464, 465, 466, 470, 471, 472, 473, 485, 486, 488, 489, 490, 492, 493, 494, 495, 496, 497, 498, 499

74(F) Squadron
Base: RAF Wattisham
Formed: 1 July 1984
Disbanded: 1 October 1992
Aircraft used by Squadron: ZE350–364; XT891, 892, 895, 896, 897, 901, 905, 907, 910, 914; XV393, 401, 409, 423, 433, 460, 465, 469, 474, 487, 490, 497, 499

92 (East India) Squadron
Base: RAF Wildenrath
Formed: 1 January 1977
Disbanded: 30 June 1991
Aircraft used by Squadron: XT895, 899, 903, 908, 909, 911, 914; XV394, 402, 404, 408, 411, 412, 413, 414, 415, 418, 420, 421, 422, 424, 430, 434, 435, 437, 439, 460, 461, 462, 465,

466, 467, 468, 469, 471, 472, 476, 480, 481, 482, 483, 484, 485, 487, 488, 489, 490, 492, 496, 497, 498, 499, 501

111(F) Squadron
Base: RAF Coningsby, Leuchars
Formed: 1 July 1974
Disbanded: 1 October 1992
Aircraft used by Squadron: XT598, 857, 859, 863, 864, 865, 867, 870, 872, 873, 874, 892, 895, 912; XV401, 403, 404, 406, 409, 410, 414, 416, 419, 424, 426, 428, 429, 432, 436, 437, 476, 478, 480, 485, 486, 491, 494, 500

1435 Flight
Base: RAF Mount Pleasant, Falkland Islands
Formed: 1 November 1988
Disbanded: July 1992
Aircraft used by Squadron: XV408 (Hope), 461 (Charity), 466, 472 (Faith)

A well-worn Phantom about to depart on a live missile-firing sortie from RAF Valley in March 1983.

Index